The Little Confectioner

Also from Westphalia Press
westphaliapress.org

The Idea of the Digital University

Criminology Confronts Cultural Change

Eight Decades in Syria

Avant-Garde Politician

Socrates: An Oration

Strategies for Online Education

Conflicts in Health Policy

Material History and Ritual Objects

Jiu-Jitsu Combat Tricks

Opportunity and Horatio Alger

Careers in the Face of Challenge

Bookplates of the Kings

Collecting American Presidential Autographs

Misunderstood Children

Original Cables from the Pearl Harbor Attack

Social Satire and the Modern Novel

The Amenities of Book Collecting

Trademark Power

A Definitive Commentary on Bookplates

James Martineau and Rebuilding Theology

Royalty in All Ages

The Middle East: New Order or Disorder?

The Man Who Killed President Garfield

Chinese Nights Entertainments: Stories from Old China

Understanding Art

Homeopathy

The Signpost of Learning

Collecting Old Books

The Boy Chums Cruising in Florida Waters

The Thomas Starr King Dispute

Salt Water Game Fishing

Lariats and Lassos

Mr. Garfield of Ohio

The Wisdom of Thomas Starr King

The French Foreign Legion

War in Syria

Naturism Comes to the United States

Water Resources: Iniatives and Agendas

Designing, Adapting, Strategizing in Online Education

Feeding the Global South

The Design of Life: Development from a Human Perspective

The Little Confectioner

19th Century Candy and Cake

by H. Hueg

WESTPHALIA PRESS
An Imprint of Policy Studies Organization

The Little Confectioner: 19th Century Candy and Cake
All Rights Reserved © 2017 by Policy Studies Organization

Westphalia Press
An imprint of Policy Studies Organization
1527 New Hampshire Ave., NW
Washington, D.C. 20036
info@ipsonet.org

ISBN-13: 978-1-63391-577-0
ISBN-10: 1-63391-577-8

Cover design by Jeffrey Barnes:
jbarnesbook.design

Daniel Gutierrez-Sandoval, Executive Director
PSO and Westphalia Press

Updated material and comments on this edition
can be found at the Westphalia Press website:
www.westphaliapress.org

The LITTLE CONFECTIONER

PUBLISHED BY
H. HUEG
LONG ISLAND CITY
NEW YORK

THE
Little Confectioner

PUBLISHED BY

H. HUEG, LONG ISLAND CITY

NEW YORK

INTRODUCTION.

THE principal thing in making confectionery is to know how to boil the sugar, and its tendency to granulation while and after the boiling is done. Confectioners use two methods to determine the proper time, one is that of the common finger test, the other method is that of the thermometer. A Fahrenheit thermometer graded up to 400 degrees is generally used in confectionery. With this instrument sugar can be boiled to any degree of a uniform hardness and density. The boiling of the sugar by the finger test and the proper degree as marked on the thermometer will both be given in the recipe.

L. I. City, N. Y.   H. HUEG.

LIST OF TOOLS.

1 furnace, 1 copper boiler, 1 thermometer, 1 marble and 4 iron rods ½ inch square to go around the marble and keep sugar from running off; also a candy shears and hook, a batch and a pallet knife. These tools are needed to run business on a small scale; for wholesalers there are very handy tools in the market, such as revolving steam pans, batch warmers, drop machines, rollers, etc.

CLARIFYING.

The clarifying and boiling of sugar to the different degrees is the base or key to all sorts of candymaking.

15 lbs. sugar, 3 qts. water, 1 white of egg, which is beat up with 1 pt. water, put the whole into the boiling pan; as soon as it comes to a boil add 1 pt. water; when it rises again add another ½ pt. water; this prevents the scum from boiling into the sugar and makes it rise to the top; now is the time to take all the scum off; when done dip in your finger, and if a drop hangs from it, it is the "1" degree, called "smooth."

THE THERMOMETER.

There are three different thermometers in use, the one of Fahrenheit, (in America and England), the one of Reaumur, (in Germany and Austria), and the one of Celsius, (in France and Switzerland). Fahrenheit sets his freezing point at No. 32, the boiling point 212. Reaumur has the freezing point marked 0, and boiling point at 80. Celsius sets the freezing point at 0, and the boiling point at 100.

In this book we use one the of Fahrenheit graded up to 400 degrees. If you buy a new thermometer you will have to be careful, as thermometers vary some, which you can very easily find out by boiling a batch **or** two.

The **pe**arl is to boil to 220 degrees; the small thread 228 degrees; the large thread 236 degrees; the blow 240 degrees; the feather 242 degrees; the small ball 244 degrees; the large ball 250 degrees; the small crack 261 degrees; the hard crack 281 degrees; the caramel 360 degrees.

CRYSTALIZATION.

The articles to be crystalized should be put in pans having sides 2½ inches high. Then put in a copper or brass kettle as much water as will more than fill the pans. Then add 7 lbs. of sugar to a gallon of water and boil by the thermometer to 225 degrees; take if from the fire and let it cool until blood warm, then pour upon the goods sufficient to cover them; put them in a warm place for 10 hours, pour off the syrup and let them dry well before turning them out. The principle upon which the above is conducted is readily comprehended. When water is cold it will dissolve but a certain quantity of sugar and no more. When heat is applied it will dissolve a much greater quantity. When taken from the fire and allowed to cool the superfluous sugar that was held in solution by the heat, now begins to form itself in crystals and is deposited on the sides and bottom of the vessel, or upon the goods. Cream figs, cream dates, cream nuts can easily and without trouble be crystalized in the above manner. No cream of tartar or alcohol must be used.

SUGAR SPINNING.

Boil 1 lb. sugar, 1 gill water, little cream of tartar, 310 degrees. Any workman with ordinary ideas of symmetry, designs and perspective can produce efforts in sugar spinning which surprise themselves. All there is necessary for practice is a flat piece of glass well oiled, lay the glass onto the design you want to make. Dip your spoon in the above sugar and trace the designs, when cool put them together with caramel. Spun sugar is used for many decorative purposes, such as falling or running water, etc., this is made by dipping a docker or bunch of wires into the sugar, then hold an iron bar in your left hand, as high as you can reach, run the docker over the bar as quick as possible, letting it nearly touch the floor. Continue this until there is a skein of sugar that looks like a skein of silk, the threads can be made fine or coarse by moving the wires slow or fast.

TO SPIN A SILVER WEB.

Take 1 pt. of clarified sugar and 1 teaspoonful of lemon juice, boil in a small pan to the degree called "caramel"; the moment the sugar is ready take it off and put the bottom of the pan in cold water. As soon as the water is warmed take the pan out. This precaution will keep the sugar from discoloring. As this sugar is to represent silver you must be particularly careful not to boil it too high. Have ready a crocanth mould neatly oiled with sweet oil, then take a teaspoon and dip the shank of it in to the sugar on one side of the pan; take up a little sugar and throw the spoon backwards and forwards in the mould, leaving as fine a thread as possible. Continue to do so until the mould is quite full. You must observe that there be no blotches and that the threads be as fine as hair; you may then take it out and cover it over a custard or any other sweet, and may, if you please, raise it by spinning light threads of sugar on the top.

TO SPIN A GOLD WEB.

Proceed with a gold web exactly the same as with the silver web, only boil the sugar a moment longer.

SPUN SUGAR BEE-HIVE.

Mould 20 or 30 bees in gum paste, as near the color and shape as possible, make a hole with a pin on each side of the mouth and let them dry; make some of the wings extend as if flying. Provide a large round crocanth mould as near the shape of a bee-hive as possible, then boil the sugar as formerly instructed. Spin the sugar hot close to the inside of the mould. It must be regularly spun and very strong, the threads very fine and no blotches. When it is so, let it stand until quite cold, then turn it out of the mould on to a large dish and ornament.

IMITATION EGGS IN GRAINED SUGAR.

These only can be made with egg-shaped moulds of metal or wood. If made of the former material, the two halves must be slightly oiled before being used, and if of the latter, soaked in water and dried with a sponge afterwards, as they require to close perfectly air-tight. Only one-half of the mould must be filled with the sugar, while an assistant must be ready to instantly close the mould up and turn it round to distribute the contents equally all over the inside. To make the eggs lighter in weight some of the syrup may be drained from the interior of the eggs while they are warm by means of the small hole in the end. This opening may be stopped up with a patch of the grained sugar or the egg filled with yellow fondant cream in imitation of a yolk. The best or whitest refined sugar is used for these goods and boiled to a "soft ball," or about 240-245 degrees by the thermometer. It will be advisable for those who desire to manufacture this class of goods to use small boils in their first attempt, and only slightly grain the same, and well stir that in a drop-pan with a lip to it.

PANORAMA EGGS.

These require a special mould, extra dry starch powder, and deep starch coffers or boxes. You must make a mould of plaster of Paris as follows: Form a wall of potters clay about 2½ inches deep, into which run some soft plaster, and while it is yet soft press into it, exactly half way, an egg that has been well greased. As soon as the plaster sets remove the egg and the clay, and you have a mould with the impression of half an egg in it. Drill a small hole through the mould at the bottom of the egg empression in order to facilitate the escape of the air when the mould is in use; trim the mould nicely and smoothly on the outside. When the mould is perfectly dried fasten on the flat surface a piece of cork or wood, to serve as a handle. Now have coffers or shallow boxes, say three or four inches deep; fill these with fine dry starch powder, smooth off the top of the starch with a ruler, and with your mould print the starch; then boil your sugar to the "feather" degree, and by means of a confectioner's funnel or a small lip pan, fill your starch prints with it; sieve some starch powder lightly over the top and set it way in a moderately warm place until next day. Then gently remove the castings from the boxes, and with a soft brush carefully brush off any adhering starch. Now make a little hole in the top of the casting, drain off the syrup contained in them, after which set them for one moment on a wetted towel and then gently break away the surrounding sugar and you have half an egg— the outside crystal and the inside smooth. Now, in the pointed end of the egg, make a small hole, and in one of the half eggs construct your panorama. Place a small round piece of glass in the hole at the end and fas ten it with a little icing; join, also, another half egg to it with icing, thus forming a whole egg; conceal the joints by means of a narrow strip of gold paper, and you have a panorama egg.

A much easier way of making egg moulds is as follows: Take a sharp scissors and cut and trim the edges off a half an egg shell lengthwise, grease the shell very light, and fill it up with thin plaster of Paris; when set take off the shell, put a handle onto it, and it is ready for use. If you like to have the outside mould of an egg turn the shell over, grease them, put a pasteboard ring around it, and fill up with plaster of Paris. Very nice moulds are made by not greasing at all and keeping the shells onto the moulds.

CARAMEL ORNAMENTS.

They generally require moulds out of lead or copper in which you pour your boiling sugar, but there is a way to make these kind of ornaments without moulds, which I would like to explain.

Cut out the different parts of the ornament into pasteboard, put them onto the oiled marble, and run a plain tube of icing around the edge of the patterns; when done take out your pattern and continue until all the parts of the ornaments are done; when dry pour in your sugar, boiled to 280 degrees; when cool pick them up and put together with caramel or icing. These ornaments can be crystalized or decorated with icing gum leaves, roses, flowers, and paper leaves; you can also cast the different parts into different colors.

PAPIER-MACHE.

Soak any amount of white paper in scalding water for 1½ hour, then press the water out of it, and pound it into a smooth pulp. Now add 4oz. of glue, dissolved, and ¾ lb. powdered chalk, and make a stiff paste; this paste can be used in place of gum paste.

PASTILLAGE.

1 qt. water, 2 oz. of gum traganth; soak for 36 hours; now press it through a cloth, then add a few drops of glycerine and equal parts of icing sugar and corn starch, and make a nice paste by working it well; this paste may be used instead of gum paste.

ROCK SUGAR.

Boil 2 lbs. sugar to a crack, and stir in ¼ lb. ornamenting icing; let it cool off, turn it out, and break into suitable pieces for the construction of rocks.

ICE-CREAM CANDY.

The process of making Ice-Cream Candy is nearly the same, as far as regards boiling the sugar, as in making nearly all kinds of sticks and drops. The ingredients are as follows:

>Best Standard A Sugar..10 lbs.
>Water....................2 qts.
>Butter..................1½ lbs.
>Cream of Tartar.......1 teaspoonful.

Dissolve the sugar in the water, and put it over the fire; when it reaches the boiling point add the cream of tartar. When it has boiled ten minutes put in the butter. It will now commence to foam, and will occupy twice the space it did before, therefore care should be had to select a vessel large enough so that the boiling syrup should not run over. Now it is necessary to use the tests for boiling sugar, in order to know when the batch is done. Put your thermometer in the pan, and holding in your left hand a dipper of cold water, wet your right forefinger, and dip into the syrup, catching a little of it on your finger, and put it into the dipper of cold water. A jelly-like matter will adhere to your finger, or very likely run off it. Repeat the test every few minutes until, as you take your finger from the water, the syrup will congeal and slip from your finger in a little lump that, when pressed, will snap like glass. This is the signal that it has been boiled enough. If you look at the thermometer you will observe that it indicates 280 degrees. Pour the syrup quickly on the stone (having previously greased it). As soon as the edges begin to cool, turn them up on the middle, and continue the process until the whole mass is in a bunch; then as soon as it is cool enough to handle, put it on a hook, and pull it back and forth until it is of a snowy whiteness. While being pulled is the best time to flavor, thereby working it uniformly through the batch. Extract of vanilla or oil of lemon is the favorite. Take it from the hook and put it on the table again, and pull it out in bars, or leave it in a mass, to suit yourself. In warm weather it is difficult to keep this kind of candy, for the great quantity of cream of tartar in it renders it soft and sticky, unless kept from the air.

To make Chocolate Ice-Cream Candy, proceed as above in every particular until when the syrup is poured on the stone; mix thoroughly through it half a pound of chocolate, previously ground or powdered. It is necessary to knead this as dough is worked in order to thoroughly incorporate the chocolate in the batch. There should be enough to give the batch the same color as the chocolate, because when pulled it becomes much lighter.

STRAWBERRY ICE CREAM.

Proceed as for vanilla. When the ingredients are all in, and the batch is boiling, put in the red cochineal color until it is a little darker than a strawberry, as in pulling it always becomes lighter. Boil by thermometer to 280 degrees, or sharp crack by finger. Flavor while it is on the hook with strawberry.

VANILLA CARAMELS.

Best Standard A Sugar....6 lbs.
Glucose ....4 lbs.
Butter ....1½ lbs.
Sweet Cream ....2 qts.
Two tablespoonfuls of Ex. Vanilla.

Stir the sugar and the cream together, and when well mixed add the glucose. Put the mixture on the fire, and stir it constantly or the cream will burn. When it has boiled fifteen minutes add the butter, and commence to try the sugar with the finger test. The thermometer is of no practical value in making this kind of candy. Try the sugar with the finger every minute, and as soon as the sugar cracks sharply when pressed, remove the pan from the fire and add two tablespoonfuls of extract of vanilla, stirring it in very briskly. Then pour the syrup upon the marble. It might be well to mention that the marble must be greased before the syrup is poured on it, and for convenience, it is best to do it before commencing to boil the sugar. It will be observed that these Caramels are of an opaque appearance, consequent on using cream. When the syrup is nearly cool, crease it, or cut it into small pieces, three-quarters of an inch square. If sweet cream is not to be had, three cans of condensed milk will answer nearly as well. It should be reduced with water until of the consistency of cream.

VANILLA CARAMELS.

Best Standard A Sugar...10 lbs.
Best Butter .... 2 lbs.
Milk................... 3 qts.
One teaspoonful of cream of tartar.

Mix the milk and sugar together, and, when it commences to boil, add the cream of tartar. When it has boiled ten minutes add the butter, and commence to test it with the finger, as in the previous recipe. When it has reached the same point as before, remove it from the fire, and stir in two tablespoonfuls of vanilla very gently. Great caution must be used not to stir the mixture after it has been removed from the fire.

But while boiling it must be stirred constantly. These caramels will not be transparent, but of a cream color.

MAPLE CARAMELS.

These are made precisely as the others, except in place of standard A sugar use pure maple sugar, and proceed in the same manner as for vanilla, except that the flavor of the maple is sufficient without any other.

CHOCOLATE CARAMELS.

Best A Sugar............6 lbs.
Glucose ....4 lbs.
Butter.................1½ lbs.
Sweet Cream............2 qts.
Caraccas Cocoa Paste....1½ lbs.
Two tablespoonfuls Vanilla.

Dissolve the sugar in the cream, then add the glucose, and put it on the fire. When it has boiled ten minutes, add the butter and the cocoa paste. These caramels must be stirred very briskly while boiling, for the cream and chocolate burn very easily. A spatula is the best thing to stir with; this is a stick about two inches wide and a couple of feet long. As the boiling progresses the syrup will become thick as pudding. Try it very often with the finger test, and when it gives a sharp crack take it from the fire, add two tablespoonfuls of vanilla extract, and pour it on the marble. The vanilla should be well stirred in. When it is almost cold cut it up in squares, or crease it with a knife. These caramels sell all the year around, and in summer should be kept in a covered tin box.

When made strictly after the above recipe they are unsurpassed.

CHOCOLATE CARAMELS.

Best A Sugar............10 lbs.
New Milk ....2 qts.
Butter ....1½ lbs.
Baker's Chocolate ....1½ lbs.
One teaspoonful of cream tartar.

Dissolve the sugar and the milk together, and when it comes to the boiling point add the cream of tartar. When it has boiled ten minutes add the butter and chocolate. Stir it continually, as the milk will burn quicker than cream. When the butter and chocolate are in, try it continually with the finger test; as soon as it gives a sharp crack, remove it from the fire, stir in two tablespoonfuls of extract of vanilla, and pour it on the marble as soon as possible. Great care must be used in stirring this when not boiling, as without glucose it has a tendency to granulate on account of the milk.

PEANUT BAR.

Take of the shelled kernels 2 pounds to 1 of sugar, and pass them through a sieve, to remove the dirt and dust, and pick them over carefully to remove all bad kernels. Place them in easy reach. Take 3 pounds best A sugar, and put it dry in a kettle, and set it on the fire. Add one teaspoonful of cream tartar to the dry sugar. Stir the sugar up from the bottom with a spatula, until it has all melted. Then throw in the nuts slowly, until there is just sugar enough to cover them. Stir briskly until the nuts turn to a light brown, and then pour the batch on the marble. Pat them down flat until the mass is only an inch or an inch and a half thick, and cut them to any desired width while still warm. If the kernels are roasted to light brown first, it saves time and much work stirring, besides making better candy.

PEANUT BAR.

ANOTHER WAY TO MAKE THE SAME.

Take of any old candy, say 5 pounds, add one quart of water, and 3 pounds of glucose. Boil until syrup comes to a sharp crack, then put in the nuts until the syrup will not take any more, continualy stirring them for two or three minutes, and then dumping them out on marble. Cut when nearly cold. Roast the nuts first to a light brown.

PEANUT BAR.

Take a pan with sides 1½ inches high, fill it nearly to the top with shelled nuts. Then boil 5 pounds of A sugar in 1½ pints of water and ¼ teaspoonful of cream of tartar, until a very sharp crack, or with thermometer 300 degrees. Then pour upon the nuts, and when yet warm cut in bars. This plan does not cook the nuts, and consequently does not eat as well as either of the above. But if the nuts are roasted first, then this method makes a very good candy. Almonds, walnuts, Brazil nuts and filberts, when treated this way, make a splendid candy.

ALMOND BAR.

Take 5 pounds of best A sugar and a quarter of a teaspoonful of cream of tartar; put them dry in a kettle and stir them until the sugar has all melted. Then throw in the almonds slowly until the syrup will not cover any more. Do not neglect to stir the mixture constantly. Turn the mass on the marble, flatten it out, and cut it into bars when nearly cold. English walnuts, filberts, or Brazil nuts made in this manner sell very readily. These nuts do not need any cooking; as soon as all the nuts are in the syrup it is done.

COCOANUTS.

In selecting these nuts care should be taken to choose those in which the kernel does not adhere to the shell, as they are much the best. They are known as Carthagena nuts, and this variety is almost exclusively used by confectioners. To prepare them, the outside shell should be removed with a sharp hatchet, without injuring the kernel. Then with a spoke-shave set firmly, take off the dark skin that covers the meat. Quarter them and boil them about fifteen minutes, and they will be ready to cut up, either with a machine, if you have one, or grated on a coarse grater.

COCOANUT CAKES.

Grate, or cut with the machine five nuts; then take 5 pounds of best A sugar and 1 pint of water, and boil them until the thermometer reaches 275 degrees, or by the finger test, until the sugar gives a slight snap. Remove the syrup from the fire, and stir in the grated nuts. Then return the pot to the fire and boil it again, until, when a small quantity is taken between the finger and thumb, it will draw out like a thread. It should be stirred constantly from the time the nuts are put in. When it reaches the desired consistency, remove it from the fire, stir it gently a few times and take some out with a spoon and spread it with a fork on tins to any size you desire. These cakes can be colored by using a small quantity of the colors to be described further on. Another variety is made as follows: grate a small quantity of chocolate fine, and stir it into the mass just before removing it from the fire. This makes a very saleable article.

COCOANUT CREAM BAR.

Grate 5 nuts. Take 5 pounds of sugar and 1 quart of water, and boil them until the mercury in the thermometer reaches 260 degrees. Then put in the nuts, remove the thermometer, and let it boil about 3 minutes, stirring it all the time. Take it off the fire and stir it gently until the mass gets stiff and white. Pour it out on the marble, flatten it, and when cold, cut it into bars. This candy can be colored the same way as the Cocoanut Cakes.

CREAM FOR CHOCOLATE CREAM DROPS.

Best A Sugar............10 lbs.
Water ....2½ qts.
One teaspoonful of cream of tartar.
Mix the sugar and water together and put

it over a hot fire. When it comes to a boil, add the cream of tartar, and put in the thermometer. If it is summer boil until the mercury marks 245 degrees, as the cream must be harder, but in winter 241 degrees is hard enough. By the finger test, the syrup should be of the consistency of jelly, so that it can be rolled up in a ball. As soon as it reaches the desired heat, take the kettle off the fire instantly, and set it in a tub of cold water, or in some very cool place. While it is still warm, but not hot, stir the mass briskly with a spatula or long handled pudding stick, until it turns as white as snow, and is of a soft, creamy texture. Before it is stirred, it should be flavored with two tablespoonsful of extract of vanilla. When beginning to stir the cream as it cools, the motion should be brisk and uninterrupted, to prevent the syrup from becoming granulated, which would render it unfit for use. When it is creamed take it from the kettle, and knead it with the hands until there is not a lump left in it, and the mass is of a uniform softness. The cream is then ready for use for various purposes, and will keep a long time if kept in a covered stone jar.

CHOCOLATE CREAM DROPS.

Roll little bits of the cream described above to the size and shape of common marbles; and place them on stiff, glazed paper, to harden a little on the outside.

Put some cocoa paste or plain chocolate in a vessel, and set it in boiling water, until the chocolate is dissolved, but do not put any water into the chocolate. When the chocolate is all melted, drop the balls of cream into it, two or three at a time, and, lifting them out again with a fork, place them on the glazed paper to dry. As soon as the operation is finished, the drops should be placed in a cool place. These drops are sometimes glazed by a solution of shellac and alcohol, put on with a soft brush.

CHOCOLATE CREAM BAR.

Have a pan with sides an inch and a half high. Grease some paper and fit it neatly around the sides and bottom of the pan. Prepare some chocolate as in the foregoing recipe, and pour it into the pan to the depth of a quarter of an inch. Now take some of the cream described above, and putting it in a pan over the fire, stir it continually until it is melted, pour it into the pan on top of the chocolate, to the depth of an inch. When it has cooled a little put a layer of chocolate on the cream, a quarter of an inch deep. When it is cool the cake can be cut in bars.

COMBINATION CREAM BARS.

Take a pan of two or three inches depth, and cover it inside with greased paper as above. Pour into it half an inch of melted cream, also as above. Take the same quantity of cream, and as it melts color it a delicate pink, or red, and flavor it with strawberry. When melted, pour this on the first. Then take the same quantity of cream again, color it yellow and flavor it with lemon, and pour it on top of the other two. When it is cold cut it in halves, through the center, and put one-half on top of the other.

It is always the best plan to cover the inside of the pan with greased paper, as then you may be sure that the cake will turn out of the pan whole and unbroken.

PHILADELPHIA WALNUT CANDY.

Best New Orleans Molasses... ½ gal.
Glucose .... 2 lbs.
Water .... 1 qt.

Boil the mixture until, by the finger test, the syrup cracks. Then gradually put in the walnut kernels until the syrup will cover no more. The batch is then done, for the nuts need no cooking whatever. Turn it out and flatten it on the marble; and cut it before it gets cold.

PHILADELPHIA WALNUT CANDY.

WITHOUT GLUCOSE.

Best New Orleans Molasses....1 gal.
Water ....1 qt.

One-half teaspoonful cream tartar. Proceed in the same way as in the previous recipe. Both should be continually stirred while boiling. No cream of tartar is necessary where Glucose is used.

LEMON ACID DROPS.

Put 10 pounds of sugar and 2 quarts water in a kettle over the fire. When they come to a boil, add half a teaspoonful of cream of tartar. Put in the thermometer and let it boil until the mercury reaches 305 degrees, or, by the finger test, until the syrup gives a good hard snap. Remove the kettle from the fire and pour the contents onto the marble, so that the batch will be about a quarter of an inch thick. Take three teaspoonfuls of finely powdered tartaric acid and twenty drops of oil of Lemon, and spread them evenly on the surface of the hot sugar. Now begin to turn the edges onto the middle, repeating the operation several times, and gradually make a lump of the whole batch, and knead it like dough, so as to thoroughly dissolve the acid and get it worked into the sugar. It can now be drawn out and cut into drops with the scissors, or rolled into sticks. Lemon drops are a very popular confection, and when made as above, are of a beautiful straw color, and perfectly transparent.

LEMON DROPS WITHOUT ACID.

These drops are very simple to make and are in connection with raspberry, strawberry, banana and pine-apple, an admirable article for mixed candy. They look well and are very quickly made.

To 10 pounds of A sugar add two quarts of water and scant half a teaspoonful of cream tartar, in this place it will be well to describe accurately the different amounts or measures of cream tartar, as for instance, we say as above, a half teaspoonful it is meant that the bowl of the spoon even full with the rim. A teaspoonful would, of course, be twice as much. It is absolutely necessary that these proportions or measure should be followed with accuracy to insure success in candy making. Boil by thermometer to 305 degrees, and as soon as it is off the fire pour into it the flavoring oil, as soon as it is on the marble prepare to mark it off in squares, about three-quarters of an inch is the popular size, and while warm raise it from the marble as it will stick. Strawberry and raspberry is colored while boiling. Drop the color in when half done; do not stir it. Pineapple and banana color yellow; none of these should be very deep, but a delicate tinge.

STICK CANDY AND DROPS.

Standard A Sugar............10 lbs.
Water ....2 qts.
Cream of tartar, half teaspoonful.

Confectioners vary a few degrees in making these varieties in the winter or spring months, the degree for boiling the sugar is 305. In the extreme hot weather of the summer it is boiled to the 315 degrees, from which point the sugar changes from a beautiful transparent mass to a brown color.

Peppermint is pulled and striped with six red stripes evenly distributed around the stick. Wintergreen is also pulled, and striped with one broad and three narrow red stripes. Sassafras is also pulled and distinguished by three red broad stripes, the center stripe is pulled on the hook until it is four or five shades lighter than its fellows. Lemon is generally surrounded by four narrow white stripes, the body of the sticks are transparent. Cinnamon is colored red and as often pulled as left transparent and is striped with four narrow white lines. Pineapple is pulled and ornamented with two red stripes with a yellow between. Clove is left transparent with a slight tinge of red with an alternate white and red stripe. Banana is a transparent stick with four narrow yellow stripes, the body of the stick is sometimes tinged with yellow. Cream sticks are mostly white and flavored with vanilla.

The drops are striped exactly the same as the stick.

The above are the principal flavors used and the distinguishing characteristics that time and usage has given to the different varieties.

In boiling sugar for these varieties, depend on the thermometer, for none but old and skillful confectioners can do it without, as the sugar cracks very sharp at 290, whereas, the boiling continues in some cases to 315 degrees. When the boiling is completed turn it on the marble, and as soon as the edges become cool turn them on the center and repeat the process until the whole batch can be turned over as fast as it cools.

If wanted to make peppermint sticks, cut off a portion of the soft candy, as soon as possible, after it has been poured on the marble, say a quarter of a pound, and color it a bright red. It needs only a very small quantity of coloring matter, which, however, must be thoroughly worked in with the hands. When this is done put the colored candy in a pan near the fire, to keep warm until ready for use. Now return to the batch and cool it as rapidly as possible. When sufficiently cool to handle, put it on a hook, and draw it out until it is of a snowy whiteness. Then remove it from the hook and roll it round on the marble. Now take your colored piece, cut it into six equal strips and place them at equal distances around the batch. Now work one end of the whole down to a point, and pull it out into sticks of any desired thickness; twisting it a little to make the six stripes into a pretty spiral around the stick. The best time to flavor these sticks is while pulling the batch on the hook, and is done by simply pouring a few drops of oil of peppermint on it, and **it** will get worked in very thoroughly by the pulling. It requires a good deal of skill to make a good stick, but to make a good drop is very easy. The above process is used for all other kinds of sticks.

CUT DROPS.

In making these the learner can by degrees get accustomed to working the candy and striping it for the different varieties. If it is not striped in an artistic manner, it does not show the defects on a small drop, and if they are not pulled out to suit for drops, they can be left in unequal lengths and sold for broken candy. The writer has for a number of years discarded all machines for making these drops and used a common caramel cutter; the drops are cleaner cut and lighter than when passed through a machine. Draw out and roll the candy as if making sticks. Pass the cutter over and cut them nearly through. When cold they readily break and form a very attractive drop. If while working, the batch becomes too cold hold it over the fire and it will soon soften; the operation should be conducted in a warm room.

CREAM CANDY.

Is formed in large, irregularly flattened sticks whose surfaces are rough and uneven. The process is exactly the same as for the sticks. They are not striped, but the whole batch is colored. Vanilla is always white. Strawberry, raspberry and rose is a delicate pink. Orange is colored a pale yellow and is flavored with oil of neroli. In using this and the oil of rose great caution must be exercised on account of the intense strength, one or two drops is sufficient for a ten-pound batch of candy. Chocolate Cream of this quality is made by adding of powdered chocolate to the batch as soon as poured on the marble enough to color of a dark brown hue; add flavor with vanilla extract or oil of bitter almonds. When this is first made it is hard and brittle. Confectioners pack it away until it becomes of a soft creamy nature, from which process it derives its name.

OLD-FASHIONED MOLASSES CANDY.

Take one gallon best New Orleans molasses, add 1 pint of water. Boil at a moderate heat in a vessel that holds at least three times the quantity. Stir it briskly all the time it's on the fire. When it becomes of a pudding-like texture, try it by the finger or use a stick, by first wetting it, and then plunging it in the syrup and back to the water. If the syrup gives a good crack put it between your teeth, if it sticks to them, boil a little longer until it does not. When nearly done put in a piece of butter, say a quarter of a pound. Turn it out quickly. Cool it as soon as possible, and pull it until it gets stiff, flavor during the pulling with oil of lemon or vanilla.

LIGHT MOLASSES CANDY.

New Orleans Molasses........½ gal.
Water ....1 qt.
Molasses Sugar ....5 lbs.
Refined Sugar ....2 lbs.

Boil as above and flavor it while pulling. This kind of candy keeps admirably during the mild weather of spring and autumn.

TAFFY CANDY.

This kind of candy is made by boiling molasses, etc., exactly as in either of the foregoing receipts, and when done, pouring it into trays and pans without pulling or flavoring. It is generally marked off into small squares with a knife.

EVERTON TAFFY.

Extra "C" Sugar................5 lbs.
Water ....1 qt.
Butter ....1½ lbs.
Half a teaspoonful of cream of tartar.

Boil the sugar and water until, by the finger test, the syrup may be pressed into a hard ball; then put in a pound and a half of sweet butter. Continue the boiling until the finger test gives a sharp crack. Before pouring out, flavor with lemon oil. This is a favorite kind of candy, and sells readily.

CHOCOLATE PASTE.

Best "A" Sugar ....5 lbs.
Water ....3 pts.
Butter ....½ lb.
One teaspoonful cream tartar.
Two tablespoonfuls vanilla.
Chocolate, or cocoa paste..........1 lb.

Dissolve sugar and water, and when they come to a boil add cream of tartar. Boil until mercury shows 230 degrees, then add the chocolate and butter. Stir constantly and try it often with finger. The thermometer cannot be used to advantage. When the mass shows a soft ball, or rather when taken from the fingers it can be rolled up, it is done. Pour in the vanilla as soon as it is off the fire, and stir through the batch until it becomes quite stiff; then run it in greased pans and when cold it will cut like cheese. This is a delicious confection and sells readily.

VANILLA CREAM ALMONDS.

Take as many of the nuts as you wish to use, roast them gently over a slow fire, until they assume, when broken, a light brown color. Take of the cream as described for chocolate cream drops, roll it smooth to about a quarter of an inch thick. Cut in strips one inch wide and wrap each nut smoothly and evenly in a piece of the cream; lay them away for two or three hours to harden, then crystallize them by the process described.

CHOCOLATE CREAM ALMONDS.

Having roasted the nuts as described above, take sufficient of the cream, put in a pan and gently melt it by constantly stirring. Then having some melted chocolate pour in enough to give the mass a dark brown appearance, then pour upon the marble, and when blood warm knead it with the hands until it is soft. Then proceed as described for Vanilla Cream Almonds.

ROSE CREAM ALMONDS.

Having roasted the nuts as for the two preceding, take sufficient of the cream, melt it as described above, not forgetting to keep it in motion, color it a beautiful pink by the addition of a few drops of the red coloring, and two or three drops oil of rose. Turn it out and knead it as above, and proceed to envelope the roasted meats. Crystallize, etc. The above process is by far the best for those who wish a delicious cream almond. But skilled confectioners employ an entirely different formula that would be exceedingly difficult for an inexperienced person to successfully follow, however plain and simple the directions.

CREAM WALNUTS.

Take of the meats of the English walnut only the halfs that are entire. Spread of the cream before mentioned, as for cream drops, on the inner side of the meat to one-quarter inch in thickness, then imbed the other half of the meat without covering the outside. Crystallize same as for nuts.

CREAM DATES AND FIGS.

Are made by simply removing the stone from the date and filling up with cream. If the figs are very large they should be cut in half. Crystallize same as for nuts.

SARSAPARILLA TAFFY.

To 5 pounds of extra "C" sugar, add 1 quart of water, half a teaspoonful of cream of tartar, half pint of molasses. Boil by thermometer to 305 degrees, and when taken from the fire add 10 drops each of sassafras and wintergreen oils, do not stir in the flavors.

CINNAMON TAFFY.

To 5 pounds of "A" sugar add 1 quart of water, half teaspoonful cream of tartar. While boiling color to a bright red with the cochineal color. Boil to 305 degrees by thermometer, and when done add 10 drops of oil cinnamon.

CANDIED NUTS.

Take any quantity of the shelled nuts, English walnuts, Brazil nuts, filberts or almonds, as preferred.

Boil sugar, say, 5 pounds to 1 quart of

water, half teaspoonful of cream of tartar to 300 degrees by thermometer, take it from the fire and drop in the nuts, a few at a time, and lift out with a fork on tins or cold marble.

ROCK CANDY.

This is a very simple and at the same time interesting process. It can be made in very small quantities, and all that is necessary is a kettle having its sides flaring or wider at top than bottom, in order that the crystallized sugar may be taken out in the same shape as the vessel. Perforate the sides of the kettle with minute holes three inches apart, then run a thread through each hole in order that the sugar may form the crystal on the thread instead of all on the bottom and sides. Cover the outside with a thin coat of beeswax and resin to keep the syrup from running out of the holes.

Take sugar in the proportion of 10 pounds to 3 quarts of water. Boil by thermometer to 220 degrees. It is now nearly boiled sufficient. Take a common skimmer and after passing it through the syrup, blow through the holes. If the syrup leaves the skimmer in light feathery particles it is done. Then pour it in the kettle prepared to receive it, and keep it in a very warm room for ten or twelve hours, examine and if the crystals are heavy enough to pour off the surplus syrup and let them dry.

CRYSTALLIZATION.

This operation consists simply in enveloping confections in a thin coating of crystals whose glistening appearance greatly adds to their beauty and has the advantage of rendering them almost impervious to the action of the atmosphere. The articles to be crystallized should be put in pans having sides two and a half inches high. Then put in a copper or brass kettle as much water as will more than fill the pans. Then add seven pounds of sugar to a gallon of water and boil by thermometer to 225 degrees, take it from the fire and let it cool until blood warm, then pour upon the goods sufficient to cover them, put them in a warm place for ten hours, pour off the syrup and let them dry well before turning them out. The principle upon which the above is conducted is readily comprehended. When water is cold it will dissolve but a certain quantity of sugar and no more. Wheat heat is applied it will dissolve much greater quantity. When taken from the fire and allowed to cool the superfluous sugar that was held in solution by the heat, now begins to form itself in crystals and is deposited on the sides and bottom of the vessel, or upon the goods. Cream figs, cream dates, cream nuts can easily and without trouble be crystallized in the above manner. No cream of tartar or alcohol must be used.

HOREHOUND CANDY.

If 5 pounds of this candy is wanted, take four one-ounce packages of the dried herb, and two quarts of water. Boil to one quart, strain and add 5 pounds of brown sugar. Boil by thermometer to 305 degrees, or to a hard snap. When done, pour upon the greased marble, and mark it off in squarese, or sticks, as quick as it will retain the impression. It will be almost, or quite impossible for a new beginner to boil these hard candies to perfection, without a thermometer, as the candy will crack at 280 degrees, whereas, the boiling is continued 25 degrees higher, and requires large experience to determine with accuracy, when the sugar reaches the desired point without the instrument, but with it no one need make a mistake.

COUGH CANDY.

THE MOST POPULAR EVER MADE.

One tablespoonful Elecampane.
One tablespoonful powdered Licorice Root.
One tablespoonful powdered Wahoo bark of the root.

Oil of Gaultheria..............8 drops.
Oil of Anise...................8 drops.
Laudanum ....30 drops.

To 10 pounds of good brown sugar, add two quarts of water, half teaspoonful cream of tartar. Boil by thermometer to 305 degrees. Turn the syrup on the marble as soon as possible, spread evenly over its surface the above articles. Turn up the edges and work the whole evenly through the mass by kneading as in bread making. It is generally cut in drops, but can be rolled in sticks, of two ounces each. If in sticks, it keeps better pulled, and also increases in bulk.

SPONGE SUGAR OR SPANISH CANDY.

Having made a wooden frame 12 or 16 square, and 4½ deep, place it on a wet slab or wooden bench. Take 7 pounds of loaf sugar, 1 quart of water, half teaspoonful of cream of tartar. Boil to the caramel degree or first snap indicated by thermometer by 280 degrees. Previous to which take three-quarters of a pound of fine powdered white sugar, mix the white of two eggs, beat it well until its stiff. When the sugar comes to the degree required put in any flavoring you desire, or color, take it off, pour your icing in, and immediately agitate the whole quickly with the spatula. In two or three minutes it will rise to the edge of the pan, let it fall again and continue stirring, as soon as it begins to rise the second time instantly pour it in the frame. Many fail at this process from pouring out at the first rising, which on the slab becomes perfectly flat and heavy. When cold remove it by passing a fine string or long pallet knife under it.

POP CORN BALLS.

Pop the corn, avoiding all that is not nicely opened. Place half bushel of the corn on the table or in a large dripping pan; put a little water in a kettle with one pound of sugar and boil as for candy, until it becomes quite waxy in water when tried as for candy; then remove from the fire and pour into it six or seven tablespoonfuls of thick gum solution, made by pouring water boiling hot upon gum arabic over night or some hours before. Now pour the mixture upon different parts of the corn, putting the hands upon the corn, lifting up and mixing until the corn is all saturated with the candy mixture. Then with the hand press the corn into balls, being quick lest it sets before you get through. This amount will make about 100 balls if properly done, white or brown sugar may be used.

GUM ARABIC DROPS.

Take 6 pounds of white gum arabic, dissolve in three quarts of water, over a slow fire, stirring it constantly from the bottom, until all is entirely melted, then strain and press it through a strong coarse cloth or seive, into a clean basin. Now add 4 pounds white pulverized sugar and 1 pint of orange flower water or other flavor. Place it over a slow fire and stir it constantly until it boils up, then remove it from the fire, let it stand a short time to settle, remove the scum and pour in moulds. Place them in the drying room at a temperature of 70 degrees for one day. Then turn them out, brush them clean and crystallize.

A GOOD COUGH CANDY.

Tincture Lobelia ....1 oz.
" Squills ....1 oz.
" Blood Root ....1 oz.
" Opium ....1 oz.

To 7 pounds A sugar add 1 quart of water.

Boil by thermometer to 305 degrees. Then put in tinctures and when it again reaches 300 degrees it is done. Cut in squares, or rolled in sticks; it sells equally well.

CHOCOLATE BON BONS.

Finest assorted gum arabic, 2 ounces.
Icing sugar, 2 pounds.
Chocolate, 4 ounces.
Whites of 2 eggs.
Flavor with vanilla.

Dissolve the gum in a gill of hot water and strain through a piece of muslin, then add the essence of vanilla, add icing sugar until the mass is quite stiff.

Melt the chocolate with a tablespoonful of water. Work it very smooth with a spoon, and stir in the whites of two eggs and icing. Fill a funnel shaped bag, with a tin tube attached to it having a quarter inch nozzle, with the white vanilla cream preparation, and push it out on a large sheet of paper covered with fine sugar. As the contents are forced out with the right hand cut with a knife the size of a large pea; as fast as a sheet of paper is filled it should be laid on a baking platter in the oven for 10 minutes to dry the outside. Next dip the white balls in the chocolate icing, holding one at a time on a fork, then lay them on wire to dry.

COFFEE AND COGNAC BON BONS.

Take 2 ounces of fine white gum arabic soaked in a gill of hot water and afterwards strained. Two pounds icing sugar, 2 ounces essence of coffee, half a gill of cognac brandy and the whites of 2 eggs.

First work the gum, brandy and enough of the icing into an elastic paste, as directed in chocolate and vanilla. Next prepare the royal icing by working the whites of two eggs, essence of coffee, and some of the sugar, so as to produce a stiff bodied yet somewhat liquid royal icing. These two foregoing preparations are to be used for the composition of these bon bons in exactly the same manner as indicated for the manufacture of those described in No. 1.

ITALIAN CREAM CHOCOLATE.

Best A Sugar..................5 lbs.
Glucose ....1 lb.
Sweet cream ....1 qt.
Cocoa paste ....1 lb.

Mix sugar and cream and when done add glucose; when the batch is well boiling add the cocoa paste. Boil until it reaches the ball degree or when it is tried by the finger the syrup can be rolled up. Take it from the fire and with the spatula stir until it creams, and then turn it out in moulds or pans. Flavor with a few drops of oil of bitter almonds or vanilla. This should be agitated continuously to prevent the cream and chocolate from burning. If glucose is not handy cream of tartar can be substituted, one teaspoonful will be sufficient.

ITALIAN CREAM WHITE.

Best A sugar..................5 lbs.
Water ....1 qt.
Cream of Tartar, ½ teaspoonful.

Boil to ball and cream it in the copper with spatula.

POWDER SUGAR.—RED.

One pound of sugar is passed through the seive to free it from the powder, which done, it is put in a sugar pan and warmed slightly, stirring it with the hand. As soon as it gets warmed, some cochineal coloring is gradually introduced, and the sugar is poured on a large sheet of paper rubbed between the hands until all is thoroughly colored of a delicate red hue. This done, it is spread over another sheet of paper and dried in the drying closet.

YELLOW POWDER SUGAR.

One ounce of hay saffron is put in a sugar pan with a gill and a half of water, a small lump of alum about size of a hazel nut, and half an ounce of sugar. The pan is set on the fire and allowed to boil for 5 minutes, then strained through a napkin. Proceed same as for red.

GREEN POWDER SUGAR.

This sugar is prepared in same manner as the red, only replacing the cochineal by some spinach green or some green office color.

SPINACH GREEN.

A small basket full of spinach is washed, pounded and pressed well in small quantities through a coarse cloth twisted at both ends, thus all the water is pressed out and put in a sugar pan which is set on the fire. As soon as the liquid begins to curdle it is poured through a sieve, so as to drain off the water, preserving only the coloring matter, which remains in the sieve. It is then taken off with a spoon and left covered on ice, keeping it for after use.

POISONOUS COLORS.

The following is a list of substances which should never, under any circumstances, be used for coloring confectionery, ice cream or any article of food whatever:

Red.—Red lead, minimum oxides of lead, cinnabar, vermillion sulphide of mercury, aniline red, which is liable to contain arsenic.

Blue.—Blue verdita, carbonate of copper and calcium.

Green.—Emerald green, Scheele's green, arsenite of copper, Reainans green, cobalt and zinc green verditer, carbonate of copper.

Yellow.—Chrome yellow, chromate of lead, orpieent, sulphate of asenic, patent yellow, Tower's yellow, Cassel's yellow, iodide of lead.

COLORS THAT MAY BE USED WITH SAFETY.

Red.—Carmine, cochineal, Brazil wood, madder.

Blue.—Powdered Prussian blue in the soluble form as sold by respectable druggists.

Yellow.—Turkey yellow berries, Persian yellow berries, quercitron, fustic, saffron, gambage is sometimes used for coloring. But while this substance can hardly be said to be poisonous in the quantities likely to be used, it would be better to abandon the use of it altogether, and substitute the turkey or Persian yellow berries, which give a beautiful and brilliant color, and one quite free from danger.

Green.—Sap green, or a mixture of Prussian blue, with any of the yellows above mentioned.

Purple.—Purple colors may be produced

by the mixture of blues with the various red colors.

A decoction of logwood gives also a good violet or purple color.

Orange.—This may be produced by mixtures of any of the reds with the yellows. Vary the proportions according to shade desired.

TO MAKE THE VARIETIES OF COLOR.

RED.
Powdered Cochineal ....4 oz.
Powdered Alum ....4 oz.
Salts Tartar ....4 oz.
Molasses ....1½ pts.
Cream of Tartar..............6 oz.
Water ....1 qt.

Put all in a copper pan and boil only long enough to dissolve the acids. Then strain through Swiss muslin.

YELLOW.
Saffron ....4 oz.
Alcohol ....16 oz.

After it has stood for one week, filter for use.

BLUE.
Powdered Prussian blue, in the soluble form, as sold by druggists, one dram, and two ounces of water.

BON BONS.

This name is given to that class of goods produced from cream, as described in the manufacture of chocolate cream. The different varieties of shape, color and flavor are nearly all produced from the same formula.

In the first place it is necessary to have an apparatus to mould the forms of the different varieties. The impressions are made in fine pulverized starch, which is put on boards usually two feet long by sixteen inches wide, having sides one and a half inches high, which are filled with the light starch and struck off even with the edges by a straight flat stick. The models of the bon bons are usually made from plaster of Paris, and are glued on a flat board about one or one and a half inches apart. When starch is ready the impressions are made by gently pressing the moulds that are fastened to the board their full depth in the starch until all are full. Now, having all ready, the cream must next be prepared to pour in the impressions.

VANILLA CREAM BON BONS.

Take of the cream previously described, pour a sufficient quantity in a small copper pan and put it over the fire. Stil it until melted, then add the vanilla flavor. It is now ready to pour in the moulds. Confectioners use a funnel shaped vessel holding about a quart, with a handle at the upper end, and a hole a quarter of an inch in diameter at the small end, a long plug with a sharp point is fitted that can easily be moved up or down to regulate the flow of the cream. This is filled with the cream, the plug prevents its escape or dripping, and by gently lifting the plug the cream can be poured in each depression and shut off continuously until all are filled. Let the cream remain until hard enough to handle without crushing, then empty the moulds, starch and contents in a sieve, and gently agitate until all the starch is removed. Lay the bon bons in a moderately warm place for two or three days to harden, then they may be crystallized.

Lemon and orange bon bons are made by simply using the oil or extract. An addition to the above may be made by mixing with the cream some of the finely grated outer rinds of the fruit.

ALMOND BON BONS.

Take a small quantity of the kernels, roast them over a slow fire until of a brown color. When cold put them in a mortar and pound them to a coarse powder, then incorporate them in the melted cream which should have a few drops of water added and three or four drops oil bitter almonds.

CHOCOLATE BON BONS.

When the cream is on the fire stir in sufficient of finely powdered chocolate and extract of vanilla to flavor, and only enough chocolate to give the desired color.

SIMPLE SYRUP FOR SODA WATER.

This is the ground work or base for all the different varieties of flavors. The writer has by long experience found that 13 pounds of refined granulated sugar to each gallon of water, is the proper quantity to be used. Boiling only sufficient to totally dissolve the sugar. The white of one egg beaten to a froth and incorporated with the sugar adds to its clearness. What impurities remain in the sugar will rise to the surface and must be skimmed off. Strain while hot through a fine collender or piece of new flannel, add one pint of glucose to each gallon of syrup. It prevents crystallization and adds to its foaming qualities when drawn from the fountain. It ought to be kept in a cool place.

RASPBERRY SYRUP.

Take any quantity of the fully ripe fruit, place them in a tub, and with a spatula with a sharp point, bruise the fruit by stirring it briskly after the skin has been broken, let them remain for two or three hours and then in a bag made of strong flannel put the bruised berries, and let the juice of its own accord run out in a suitable vessel. Mix one-half ounce of acetic acid in 3 ounces of water, and add to each gallon of the juice. Then to each gallon of the juice add 13 pounds of granulated or crushed sugar and dissolve it by gentle heat not to exceed 125 degrees by thermometer, while still warm this may be bottled and corked for future use.

STRAWBERRY SYRUP.

This fruit has a more firm texture than the raspberry, and therefore requires more force to express the juice. Proceed in same manner as for raspberry with the exception of beating the berries to a pulp, then let them stand two or three hours, after which put them in the bag and after all the juice has run out, put the bag between two boards and express the remaining juice, then add the same quantity per gallon of acetic acid, and 14 pounds of granulated sugar to one gallon of juice. Melt by gentle heat to 212 degrees by thermometer, and while still warm pour in jugs or bottles and cork tight for future use.

PINEAPPLE SYRUP.

This fruit has still greater firmness of texture than the strawberry, and requires more labor to reduce it to a fine pulp. A tub with a strong bottom and a spatula with a flat surface at the end, to pound the fruit will be found well adapted for the purpose. After laying for an hour or two the fruit should be expressed by powerful pressure.

The common cider press will answer. Add 14 pounds of granulated or crushed sugar to each gallon of juice, and a little of the acetic acid described for raspberry and strawberry. This juice should be allowed to reach the boiling point in order to acquire good keeping qualities. If the syrup should be too heavy when cold reduce as wanted to use, with water. Strain through a fine collender or new flannel.

PINEAPPLE SYRUP.
ARTIFICIAL.

To simple syrup add sufficient of the extract of pineapple to give it the required flavor.

This extract very closely resembles the true flavor of the fruit, which is not the case with most of the chemical extracts.

SARSAPARILLA SYRUP.

To simple syrup add sufficient of the following to suit the taste. Twenty drops each of wintergreen and sassafras oils in a wine glass full of alcohol. The syrup should be a dark brown color, to obtain which, use burnt sugar or extract of licorice. The former is always preferred. This makes a very popular flavor and most soda drinkers prefer it quite strong of the extract.

CREAM SYRUP.—No. 1.

This syrup is made sometimes by simply keeping a supply of pure cow's cream on the ice and use it as occasion requires. But the writer's objection to this method is the excessive foaming as soon as the soda is drawn on it.

No. 2.

A very acceptable syrup is made from condensed milk. It gives better satisfaction than any other form. Reduce the condensed milk to the consistency of cream by the addition of a little water, then add an equal quantity of simple syrup. Its keeping qualities are superior to any other form of cream syrup.

No. 3.

In order to give everybody their choice, the writer will add the following—when it is not possible to obtain the pure cream or condensed milk, this substitute will answer very well:

Beat the whites of two eggs with the

yolk of one to a froth, after which add one pound of pulverized sugar, then add gradually one pint of rich fresh milk, and stir until all the sugar is dissolved, then strain through a fine sieve.

IMITATION CREAM SYRUP.

Three fluid ounces fresh oil of sweet almonds, two ounces powdered gum arabic and nine ounces of water; then dissolve one pound of white sugar by gentle heat, strain, and when cool, add the white of two eggs. Put in bottles well corked, in a cool place. This will keep well, and is an excelent substitute for cream.

CHOCOLATE SYRUP.

Take of good quality cocoa paste, same as used for caramels, say one-half pound; if that is not at hand, Baker's chocolate will answer or a good quality of sweet chocolate. Melt in a vessel that sits in boiling water; after it has melted and while hot, add, by very small quantities, simple syrup, stirring meanwhile to incorporate the two together, until a sufficiency is added to give the whole a dark brown appearance. When cold add the vanilla flavoring.

COFFEE SYRUP.

Pure ground Java coffee, one-half pound; pure Mocha coffee, one-half pound; water, one gallon; sugar, ten pounds. Place the coffee in a stone jar or jug, heat the water to the boiling point, pour it on the coffee, tightly close the mouth of the vessel, and when cold add the sugar, then filter with very slight heat to facilitate the solution.

GINGER SYRUP.

Fluid extract of ginger, two ounces; sugar, four ounces; carbonate of magnesia, one ounce; simple syrup, one gallon. The extract of ginger is rubbed in a mortar with the carbonate of magnesia, and afterwards to this mixture is added the sugar, and thoroughly mixed. This is then added to the syrup, and the whole is heated, but not boiled, and the syrup filtered. This gives a bright, clear syrup.

SHERBET SYRUP.

Lemon syrup, one part; pineapple syrup, one part; vanilla syrup, three parts.

ORGEAT SYRUP.

Simple syrup, one gallon; extract of vanilla, one ounce; extract of bitter almonds, one-half ounce.

TRUE SYRUP OF ORGEAT.

Take four ounces of bitter almonds, two ounces of sweet almonds, blanch them by pouring hot water over them, remove the dark skins, pound in a mortar to a firm paste, and gradually add one quart of simple syrup. Strain through a fine collender.

IMITATION STRAWBERRY SYRUP.

To one gallon of simple syrup add 4 ounces German cherry juice, tincture of orris root one ounce, citric acid six drachms, strawberry flavor three drachms.

IMITATION RASPBERRY SYRUP.

Exactly as the foregoing with the exception of substituting raspberry flavor for strawberry.

MILK PUNCH.

To one quart of extra heavy simple syrup add one pint each of Jamaica rum and brandy. Flavor with two teaspoonsful of the extract made by pounding in a mortar one ounce of mace in eight ounces of the alcohol, pour this syrup in the glass and add sufficient of ordinary cream syrup.

WINE SYRUP.

Catawba, hock, claret and other wines. Having made a very heavy simple syrup of 16 pounds of sugar to the gallon. Then prepare as small a quantity as is needed by using an equal quantity of the wines and the syrup. When the syrup is about to be put on the fire add a half teaspoonful of cream of tartar to each gallon of syrup to prevent crystalization.

ESSENTIAL OILS AND EXTRACTS.

The oils usually employed in the manufacture of confections are those possessing an agreeable aromatic flavor, and are generally used in their original strength without being reduced except with alcohol. It is absolutely necessary that they should be pure and fresh. More particularly with the oils of lemon and peppermint. They are more popular than most others and therefore more frequently adulterated. When not fresh or pure they partake of the flavor of turpentine and are particularly unpleasant to the taste.

Extracts are but simple mixtures of the oils with alcohol which should be of sufficient strength to cut the oil and effect a perfect combination. Tinctures are made by pounding or macerating the articles and mixing with alcohol.

The following proportions of oils and alcohol make a better extract than can be obtained by most of the preparations manufactured for sale. Confectioners and families will find it to their interest to manufacture their own extracts from these recipes.

For practical use in flavoring candies or for household purposes, no color need be added to the extracts. It is indispensable that in the manufacture of white goods the extracts should be as free from color as possible.

EXTRACT OF ANISE.

Anise oil .... 1 ounce.
Alcohol .... 1 pint.

EXTRACT OF CLOVES.

Oil of clove .... 2 ounces.
Alcohol .... 1 pint.

EXTRACT OF CINNAMON.

True Ceylon oil............. 1 ounce.
Alcohol .... 1 pint.

EXTRACT OF BITTER ALMONDS.

Oil of bitter almonds....... 2 ounces.
Alcohol .... 1 pint.

EXTRACT OF GINGER.

Green Jamaica ginger, cut fine, 8 ounces.
Alcohol .... 1 pint.
Let it stand for one month, then filter.

EXTRACT OF SARSAPARILLA.

Oil of sassafras .... 2 ounces.
Oil of wintergreen .... 2 ounces.
Alcohol .... 1 pint.

Powdered cayenne pepper...4 ounces.
Alcohol ....1 pint.
Let it stand for a week, then filter.

EXTRACT OF VANILLA.

This exceedingly fine flavor is very difficult to procure in its pure state, owing principally to the high price of vanilla. The extract as usually sold by first-class drug houses contain an adulteration from the Tonka bean, an article that in flavor greatly resembles that of the true vanilla. Confectioners prefer in all cases to make their own extracts, this one in particular, as it is then free from all useless coloring matter, a very important point when it is used in white goods. In selecting beans very great care should be exercised, only the freshest should be purchased, they will be found to have a soft, dark pith, which oozes out when cut. Following are the true formula for making and using the extract with and without the tonka:

No. 1.

Vanilla beans ....2 ounces.
Alcohol ....6 ounces.
Water ....4 ounces.

Cut the bean one-eighth of an inch in length and macerate them in a mortar, if one is not handy they will do very well only cut. Put them in a glass vessel and let them stand two or three weeks. The extract will be found of a delicate brandy color and fine flavor.

No. 2.
VANILLA AND TONKA EXTRACT.

Vanilla .... 4 ounces.
Tonka .... 1 pound.
Alcohol .... 2 quarts.
Water .... 1 pint.

Chop or pound the beans and put them in the alcohol and water for three weeks, strain through cambric and put in tight corked bottles for use.

TO USE THE PURE VANILLA BEAN.

Take of equal parts powdered sugar and vanilla beans, macerate in an iron mortar until the whole is of a uniform fineness, put in an airtight vessel and use it dry. It is certainly the very best way to obtain the whole of the delicate flavor of the bean.

TO MAKE A SUPERIOR VANILLA EXTRACT FROM DRY VANILLA BEANS.

The following recipe for making the extract is known to but few persons, and has saved the writer many hundred dollars, and at the same time has produced an extract superior in every particular from the old way. As soon as the vanilla bean becomes dry and brittle, it can be purchased for half the price of the fresh bean. And under this process yields a flavor in many cases superior to the fresh bean treated as formerly. To three-quarters of a pound of the dry vanilla bean, cut very fine, add half a gallon of hot water, let it simmer a few minutes and then put it in a moderately warm place for 24 hours. Then add one-half gallon of best alcohol, after standing a week strain it, and it is ready for use. Six ounces of tonka beans added to the above gives additional strength, but it destroys a portion of the delicate flavor peculiar to the vanilla bean alone.

EXTRACT OF LEMON.

Pure oil of lemon..........2 ounces.
Alcohol ....1 pint.

An improvement to the above, for ice cream and household purposes, consists of cutting the yellow rind from a half dozen lemons, macerate it and put it in the alcohol, two or three days before mixing with oil. Be careful and not remove the white skin that underlies the yellow, for it has a very bitter disagreeable taste.

EXTRACT OF PEPPERMINT.

Hotchkiss' pure oil of peppermint, 2 ounces.
Alcohol ....1 pint.

EXTRACT OF WINTERGREEN.

Oil of wintergreen..........1 ounce.
Alcohol ....1 quart.

ARTIFICIAL FRUIT ESSENCES.

Artificial fruit essences, such a banana, strawberry, raspberry, pineapple, etc., are made from chemical compounds, by processes too complicated for the purposes of this work. They can be purchased of respectable druggists at much less cost than to manufacture on a small scale.

ICE CREAM.

From Pure Cream—Vanilla.

Pure fresh cow's cream.....6 quarts.
Powdered sugar ....24 ounces.
Extract of vanilla, only enough to give a delicate flavor, should be used. This cream does not require to be boiled, it will, with proper freezing, increase seventy-five per cent.

ICE CREAM.

Fresh Cream ....6 quarts.
Powdered and granulated sugar.24 oz.
Glucose ....1 pound.
The glucose renders it very smooth and should be first dissolved in the cream, then the sugar is added. No boiling is necessary.

ICE CREAM.

Fresh cream ....6 quarts.
Powdered or granulated sugar..28 oz.

The yolks of four eggs and the whites of twelve beaten to a froth, then incorporated with the sugar and added to the cream, makes a splendid ice cream, but does not increase the product as much as the two foregoing recipes.

CHOCOLATE ICE CREAM, FROM PURE CREAM

Fresh cream ....6 quarts.
Powdered or granulated sugar..30 oz.
Cocoa paste or sweet chocolate..½ lb.

The chocolate must be of good quality to insure success, as this is the most difficult of all flavors to make properly. Take a common earthen bowl of six quarts capacity, put it in hot water, melt the chocolate therein, after which add the sugar. When the two are thoroughly mixed they will grain. Then add the cold cream, a very small quantity at a time, say a tablespoonful. After it is worked in, a little more may be added, soon a smooth paste will be formed, which should be kept in that condition, by constant stirring, until the cream is all in. It should then be put in a cooler, and when cold freeze. The quantity of chocolate to use for the above amount of cream varies with the quality, consequently, after one or two trials, the amount can be definitely ascertained. Flavor with vanilla.

LEMON ICE CREAM FROM PURE CREAM.

Pure fresh cream..........6 quarts.
Powdered or granulated sugar..30 oz.
Good sized lemons...............4.

Grate the yellow rind off the lemons, boil it in half pint of milk long enough to reduce it to one and one-half gills, or put the grated rinds in a gill of alcohol an hour or two before using, or grate the lemons on a piece of hard lump sugar and use the sugar, but care must be taken lest there may be yet too much sugar which gives a very disagreeable flavor after eatin. Put all together and then squeeze the juice of two of the lemons, add a few drops of essence of lemon, strain all through a collender or piece of flannel in the freezer. Sometimes it will require five lemons and at other times only three, according to size and thickness of rind. A good way to do, if there is much business, is to prepare the flavor in sufficient quantities to last two or three weeks. It saves much time in straining and preparing when every moment is valuable.

STRAWBERRY AND RASPBERRY ICE CREAM, FROM PURE CREAM.

Pure cream ....6 quarts.
Granulated sugar ....24 ounces.
Ripe berries ....1 quart.

Macerate the berries and put one pound of sugar on them. Let them stand for two or three hours, the longer the better, then put them in a flannel bag and then gently press the juice. Do not use too much force. When the juice is ready, if it requires more sugar, add it until its taste is agreeable. Mix with the cream, if, when al' is ready, the flavor of strawberries is not prominent enough, then add of the essence of strawberry, sufficient. Color with cochineal or carmine.

CUSTARD ICE CREAM.

Fresh new milk............12 quarts.
Granulated sugar..........52 ounces.
Eggs ....48.

Beat the eggs to a froth and then add sugar to the eggs. Stir until the sugar is well incorporated with them. Next put the milk on the fire and constantly stir until it boils, using great caution lest it burn. Then pour the boiling milk on the sugar and eggs, stirring them altogether. Now put the whole over the fire, and after stirring half a minute, not any more, or just enough to thicken it slightly. When it is done, strain it and put in a cooler. When thoroughly cold, add the flavoring and freeze.

CUSTARD ICE CREAM.
IMPROVEMENT.

Fresh new milk............6 quarts.
Eggs ....24.
Granulated sugar..........52 ounces.
Fresh cream...............6 quarts.

Proceed with the eggs and milk as in the foregoing, and when all is ready for the freezer, add six quarts of rich cream.

This makes a splendid ice cream, not so rich as pure cream, which many persons cannot eat on that account. There are others who do not like custard because of so many eggs. This strikes a happy medium and is very popular.

ICE CREAM CHEAP.

Pure milk.................6 quarts.
Granulated sugar..........24 ounces.
Oswego corn starch........8 ounces.

Dissolve the starch in one quart of milk, then mix all together and just simmer a little, not boil; flavor to taste.

BISQUE ICE CREAM.

Mix one-half dozen dried maccaroons and one-third pound of sugar to each quart of cream. The maccaroons to be pounded fine and dissolved in a portion of the cream, then add the remainder, strain and freeze.

PARISIAN COFFEE ICE CREAM.

Make a half pint of very rich, strong, Mocha coffee, and add one quart of fresh, rich cream, one-half pound of pulverized sugar, and one dessert spoonful of vanilla. Beat the yolks of eight eggs very light, and add them to the mixture. Place the whole on a moderate fire, stirring continually until it thickens, with a wooden spoon or spatula; remove from the fire, strain through a hair sieve, and when nearly cold add to it half an ounce of gelatine that has been dissolved in a small quantity of milk or water; stir all well together, pour it in an ice cream mould, place a paper over the top, put on the lid and bury the mould in broken ice and salt for at least two hours; let it remain until ready for use, then take it from the ice, wipe off the mould, dip in lukewarm water and right out again; take off the lid and paper and turn it on the dish in the usual way.

COFFEE ICE CREAM.

Put one pound of pulverized sugar in a stew pan, stir in four eggs, add two quarts rich cream and one pint of strong coffee;

mix all and place on the fire, stirirng continually until it gives one boil, then remove, strain through a hair sieve; freeze when cold in an ice cream can.

CHARLOTTE RUSSE.
WITHOUT GELATINE.

One pint of pure cream, sweeten with two ounces of sugar and flavor to taste. Beat sufficient to dissolve the sugar. Beat to a stiff froth the whites of nine eggs, then add the cream; beat again, put it inside of cake and set it to cool.

This makes a filling for two moulds, one-half pint of cream and the whites of five eggs for one.

CHARLOTTE RUSSE.
WITH GELATINE—FOR ONE QUART.

Half pint of sweet cream, one gill of milk, half an ounce of isinglass, one glass Madeira wine. First line the bottom and sides of a plain mould with sponge cake, fitted closely together. Then dissolve isinglass in a half pint of water. Make a cream or custard with six yolks of eggs with the milk, one-fourth of sugar, and the dissolved isinglass on the fire. Keep stirring it until it has a thick creamy appearance, then add the wine. When cooled off whip the one-half pint of cream, sweeten it and mix with the custard. Pour it in the lined moulds and set on ice.

CHARLOTTE RUSSE.

Two quarts sweet cream, three ounces isinglass, one vanilla bean, one pint of milk, one pound of sugar and a little cinnamon. First dissolve the isinglass in milk strained through a sieve, then add sugar; let it come to a boil, remove the scum from surface, take it from the fire, whip the sweet cream to a firm substance, mix in another half pound of sugar, and flavor with pounded pulverized vanilla. Then mix the dissolved isinglass in it. Pour in a mould lined with sponge cake and place it on ice.

AMERICAN CREAM.

Ingredients, one quart of milk, four eggs, one-half box gelatine, one and a half teaspoonful of vanilla. Soak gelatine in a little cold water twenty minutes. Beat the yolks of the eggs and sugar together, let the milk come to a boil, then stir in the sugar and yolks, then the gelatine, then the whites of the eggs (having beaten them to a froth); gently stir all together, add flavoring, and pour in the mould to cool.

BLANC MANGE.

Isinglass one-four pound, rose water one-half pint, milk two quarts, sugar eight ounces, milk of almonds one-half pint; let it come to a boil, and when blood warm run in moulds.

TO MAKE MILK OF ALMONDS.

Take sweet almonds one ounce, bitter almonds three ounces, white sugar one and a half pounds, water one quart, flavor with orange flower water. Blanch the almonds by steeping them in hot water for a little time, then beat them to a mortar with the sugar, and add the water gently, lastly strain and add flavoring. Beat the almonds until they are of the consistency of cream.

OLD-FASHIONED BLANC MANGE.

Take four calves' feet, a pint and a half of thick cream, half pound of granulated sugar, a glass of wine, half a glass of rose water, and a teaspoonful of sifted mace. Boil the feet, after first cleansing thoroughly (such as have not been skinned) till all the meat drops away from the bone. Drain the liquor through a collender or sieve, and skim it well. Let it stand until next morning to congeal. Then clean it well from the sediment, and put it in a tin or metal kettle, stir into it the mace, sugar and cream, the latter having first been boiled with an ounce of broken bitter almonds. Boil hard five minutes, constantly stirring it; strain through a linen cloth into a large bowl, and add the wine and rose water. Set in cool place for two or three hours, stirring often to prevent the cream from separating from the jelly. Stir till cold, the longer the better. Wash, wipe dry, and then wet the moulds in cold water, and put in the blanc mange when it becomes very thick. After it has set quite firm in the moulds, loosen it carefully all around with a knife, and turn it out on glass plates. If the flavoring of milk of almonds is preferred, add them gradually when the mixture is ready to boil. If it sticks to the mould, set them for an instant in hot water.

BAVARIAN CREAM.

Dissolve half a package of Cox's gelatine in one quart of boiling milk, stir until it is dissolved, then add a pint of cream and sweeten to taste, add three tablespoonfuls of extract of vanilla, let it cool a little, stirring occasionally, then put it in custard cups or in a mould and leave it in a very cold place or surround it with ice; it will thicken in two hours and be ready for use.

GELATINE ICING FOR CONFECTIONS OR CAKE.

One scant stablespoonful of gelatine, dissolve in two tablespoonfuls of hot water, mix it with fine powdered sugar till quite stiff, spread with a knife smooth on the article to be iced, dip your knife in hot water during the operation. This icing does not crack after becoming dry.

ICING FOR CAKE.—No. 2.

Beat the white of eggs with sugar and add for each egg one teaspoonful of ice-cold water. This takes more sugar than when the egg is beaten to a froth, but it will keep soft for some days. To make thick icing it should be put on in two or three layers, otherwise it will be thick on the edges and thin on top; it does not pile up as in the old-fashioned icing.

EGG NOGG.

AS MADE AND DRANK IN OLD VIRGINIA.

Beat thoroughly the yolks of eight eggs with one pound of granulated sugar, with which mix one-half gallon of fresh rich milk. Then pour upon it very slowly (stirring the eggs and milk briskly) a pint and a half of best Jamaica rum; if not sweet enough add more sugar, have ready the whites of the eggs beaten to a froth, with a little pulverized sugar, stir in about one-half, put the other on top, place it on ice.

MERINGUE KISSES.

Beat the whites of four eggs until they stand alone, then beat in gradually of fine powdered sugar one pound, a teaspoonful at a time is enough, add eight drops of essence of lemon, beating the whole very hard. Lay a sheet of wet paper on the bottom of the pan, drop on it in size to suit taste, a little jelly, after putting on a little of the egg mixture first under the jelly. Then with a large spoon pile on the meringue over each lump of jelly to cover it entirely, drop it as smoothly as possible to make a good shape, set in a cool oven, when slightly colored they are done. Take them out and place them bottoms together, lay them lightly on a sieve and dry in a cool oven until the two form a ball.

GENERAL DIRECTIONS FOR LOZENGE MAKING.

A first-class lozenge is composed of a good quality of gum arabic and powdered sugar. The gum is dissolved in warm water in the proportion of one ounce of gum to two ounces of water. If the gum is powdered fine it facilitates its dissolution; from ten to twelve hours is generally long enough to effect it, of course, if left in large lumps, it takes much longer. The sugar must be of the very finest quality, and is manufactured expressly for the purpose, and is known as lozenge sugar. They can be made of the common powdered sugar as sold by grocers, but will not have the smoothness of finish attained by the first. Having dissolved the gum it must be strained to free it from the impurities. Then having a smooth marble or hard wood plank in readiness the sugar is laid on it in a heap, a hole is made in the middle and some of the gum poured in. Then with a wooden spoon gradually work in the sugar precisely as a cook does in mixing sponge for bread. When completed it may be too dry and crumble, in that case put in more gum, or it may be too soft and sticky; this may be corrected by more sugar. It should be of the proper consistency to roll smooth and cut clean. A little blue as for icing is used to bleach it white.

Having the paste already we will now proceed to get it in shape for cutting. A small piece of the dough is taken from the mass and with a common rolling pin smooth it out, frequently turning it to get both sides alike. A piece of stiff, smooth zinc is used to run under and turn it. Keep the stone well powdered with fine sugar or starch to prevent sticking. We must now have a guide to get them of a uniform thickness, procure two strips of wood an inch wide and exactly the required thickness, place them on each side of the dough and roll it to exactly their thickness. To cut them procure a tin tube about five inches in length, the small end being of the size required, and the large end should exceed that of the small by three-eights of an inch. The tapering form of the cutter gives a smooth cut and free delivery; they should be put together without lapping. Now press the cutter on the sheet and withdraw it, repeating the process until the tube is partly filled with the perfectly formed lozenge, spread on a flat board to dry, frequently turning them. In flavoring use the essential oils in their concentrated form. Cream lozenges are made by addition of a little gylcerine, say two ounces to one pound sugar. Fruit lozenges are made by mixing the jellies of fruits with the paste in equal proportions, then work in the sugar.

BURNT SUGAR.

Take of any sugar, a light brown for instance, just cover with water and boil until it turns of a dark brown color and emits puffs of smoke, remove from fire and dilute with hot water to the consistency of thin syrup. Its use is to color syrup and other preparations.

CATALOGUE AND PRICE LIST

H. Hueg & Co.,

MANUFACTURERS OF

PATENT TOOLS

FOR

Bakers, Confectioners

AND

Decorators.

CORNER THOMSON AVE. & L. I. R. R.

ONE BLOCK FROM COURT HOUSE

LONG ISLAND CITY, N. Y.

To our Customers and the Trade

In presenting our revised catalogue, we wish to call your attention to the steady growth of our business, as a guarantee of our strict reliability. In order to meet the increasing demand for our goods, we have been obliged to gradually enlarge our plant to its present capacity, and are now in a position to fill all orders wi hout delay.

We make a specialty of seamless ornamenting tubes of which we keep never less than 100,000 in stock. They are cut and bent with special tools and machinery, and are the only machine made tubes in existence. They are now used all over the world and give thorough satisfaction. Our best thanks are due to those who have favored us in the past, and our earnest endeavors will be to retain their confidence in the future. H. HUEG & Co.

IMPORTANT NOTICE.

Referring to infringements upon H. Hueg's patents.

No. 473,464,	No. 538,045,	No. 534,106,
" 554,273,	" 560,718,	" 560,719,
" 87.543,	" 42,786,	24,189,
" 542,338,	" 25,792,	" 35;433.

THE STANDARD CAKE FILLER.
Guaranteed the Best.

For filling cream cakes, corn starch puffs, eclaires, doughnuts, buns, pastry, cream rolls and all kinds of tartlets, patty pans, fancy, lunch and corn cake pans, with cream, jelly or dough.

"It Outlasts Them All."

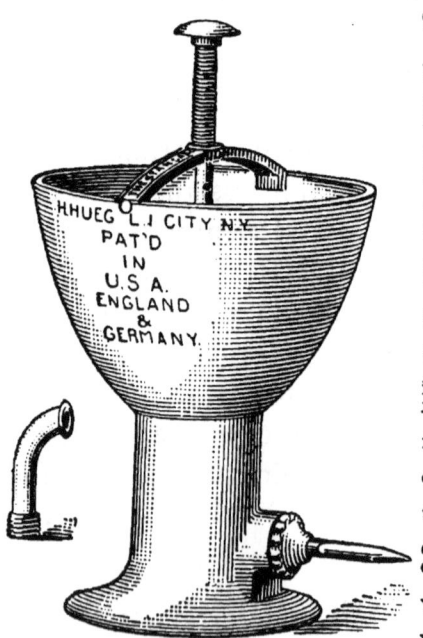

The Reasons Why?
1. Unsurpassed for simplicity and durability.
2. All parts are TINNED, therefore they cannot rust nor soil.
3. No complicated breakable castings sticking out.
4. No tin washers which are liable to rust, no complicated valves.
5. No handles, springs, nor thumb screws in your way.
6. No taking apart, no fitting nor screwing.
7. Our Filler is built on the pump system.
8. Cast in one piece, it is impossible to get out of repair.
9. It can be gauged to fill any quantity.
10. Will fill thick, thin, cold or hot material.
11. A child can operate the machine to perfection
12. All parts are interchangeable, and can be duplicated.
13. It is the only Filler with a perfect guage.
14. No taking apart when cleaning, all that is necessary is to pump the water through with force - **$5.00**

NOTE—We either make our fillers of all iron or of all tin; so whenever you see a tin hopper soldered onto a cast iron foot, make up your mind that it will not last, any mechanic will tell you that solder will not stick to cast iron any length of time.

"Merit the Basis of Honorable Success,"

IMPROVED PATENT CAKE FILLER.

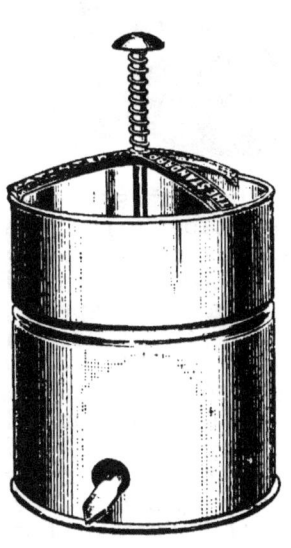

This machine is made of heavy electro plated tin with cast iron trimmings; it is made on the same style as our "Standard," will work just as well, but will not last as long; 15,000 fillers have been sold within the past six years. They are now in use all over the world. This machine is very light, easy to clean and to handle. In the hot weather it may be kept in a refrigerator so the cake can be filled with ice cold cream while the buyer waits for them. Many bakers made their fortune by following such simple ideas, $2.50

THE HANDY ROCK CAKE STAMP.

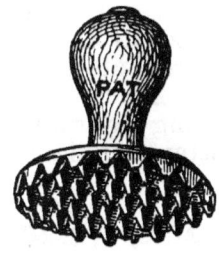

This little stamp is a great time and labor saver, it makes the cakes all alike, uniform, and prevents burnt edges; it does away with the fork, and is invaluable to any bake shop.

Sent by express, - $0.25
" " mail, - - .30

"This age demands practical men."

IMPROVED CANDY FUNNEL.

This Funnel has been on the market for the past five years. It is made of heavy electro-plated tin, and works by a spiral spring; there is no stick needed in its operation. Over 3,000 we have sold, and not a single complaint entered our office. This Funnel originally was intended for confectioners only, but lately it found its way into restaurants and hotels for laying out griddle, wheat and buckwheat cakes: for hot plates in show windows, it is invaluable, -   - $1.50

PIE STAMP.

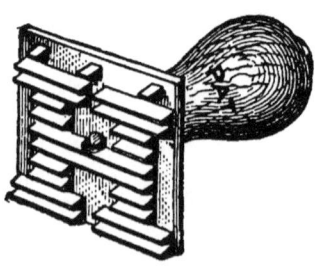

This is the most convenient Stamp; does not only stamp the initials on pies, it also punctures the cover to let the steam of the filling escape freely, which prevents running out. No trouble in selecting pies when this Stamp is used, as it shows the letter very plain.
Send by express, -   -   -   - $0.25
"   " mail, -   -   -   -   .30
Full set seven letters, A, H, L, R, M, C, P, **$1.50**

"We are originators not copyists."

IMPROVED ORNAMENTING SYRINGE.

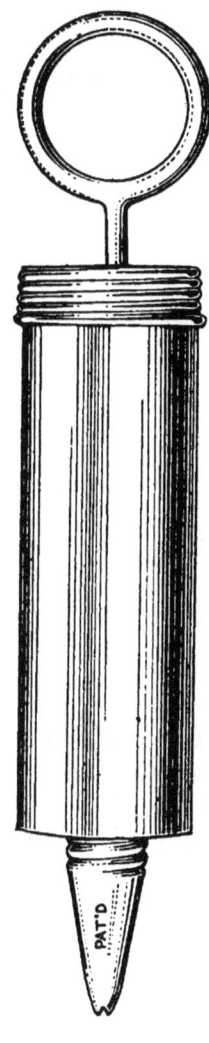

This illustration shows the simplicity of our New Ornamenting Syringe. The reasons why it should be in every bakery, hotel and confectionery;

1. No soiling of hands in filling or changing tubes.
2. No loss of time in taking out the plunger.
3. Our Syringe is filled from the bottom.
4. It works clean, is very light and easy to handle.
5. All parts are interchangeable and can be duplicated.
6. It outlasts thousands of rubber bags and bulbs.
7. It is electro-plated, japanned and tinned.
8. It is an ornament as well as an article of necessity.
9. It is very easy to clean, no taking apart.
10. The extremely moderate price places it within the reach of all.

The Syringe, only -	$1.50
With one dozen electro-plated brass tubes, -	2.50
With two dozen electro-plated brass tubes, -	3 00

Book of designs free with the above.

SHREWSBURY MOULD AND CUTTER.

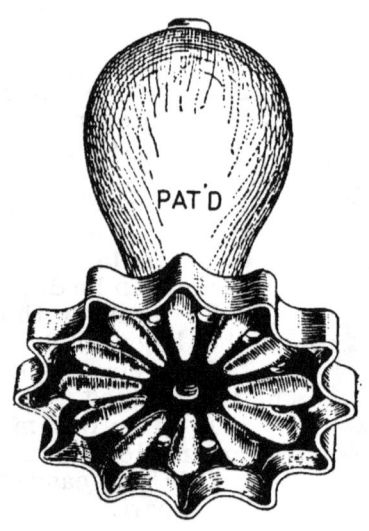

This Patent tool will cut, crimp and finish a Shrewsbury cake at one operation, and as fast as Sugar cake can be cut out; have them all perfect and uniform far superior to hand work. For very stiff doughs this tool may be used as a mould by simply unscrewing the handle.

Price, 50 Cents.

THE "BOSS" ORNAMENTOR.

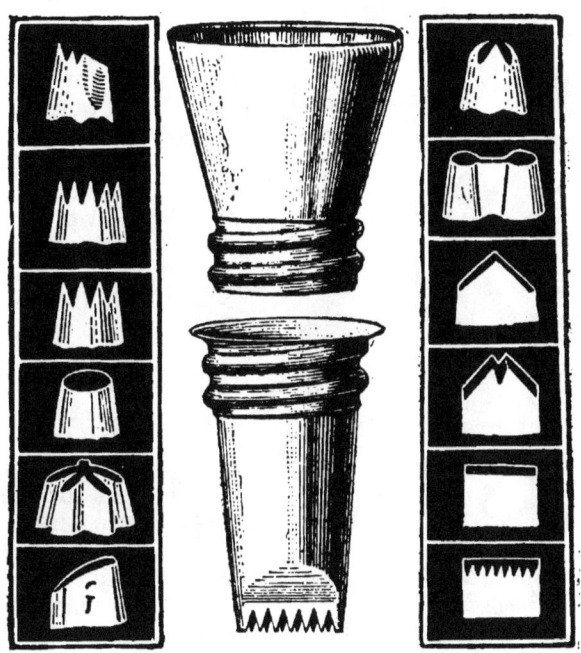

This well known tool is the old favorite of which we have sold an endless number. It consists of :
One Rubber Bag Number 2,
One Silverplated Bag Screw,
Twelve Silverplated Patent Screw Tubes,
One Book of Designs and Recipes.

Price........................$1.50.

"It is never too late to learn."

THE SCROLL MOULD.

Is a new and ingenious invention by the aid of which any person can make a large variety of the most beautiful show pieces or ornaments for show windows which formerly required skilled workmen long months of study and preparation.

At the same time its accuracy, convenience and the very short time in which show pieces can be made, render it of practical benefit to the trade.

There is no better advertising than a handsome show piece in your own window. The size of mould is 10x14, and is made of nickel-plated iron, therefore it can be used for casting, moulding as well as baking.

The most attractive ornament can be made out of caramel of different colors, also out of nougat, tragant paste, gelatine paste, macaroon, sponge cake, plaster of paris, etc.

DIRECTIONS—When all the pieces are casted, moulded or baked, stick them together with icing or caramel to the desired shape; to give the reader an idea in which shapes the scrolls can be brought, we give only a few designs on another page.

"**Difficulties. like thieves, often disappear when we face them.**"

RING MOULDS.

This mould is used in the same manner as our scroll mould, with this mould it is an easy matter to make such as: pyramids, beehives wells fruit baskets, flower baskets. and scroll show - pieces. Twelve (12) moulds make a set one being a trifle smaller, this is due to the taper of this kind of ornaments. The moulds are made of nickel-plated cast iron and can be used for casting, moulding and baking. Any size ornament can be made with these moulds from 4 inches to 4 feet high, the diameter also may be reduced from 8 inches down to 2 inches.

DIRECTIONS—One filling of the moulds will make an ornament 6 inches high; 2 fillings 12 inches high, 3 fillings 18 inches high and so on.

FOR PYRAMIDS—Take the largest ring of the largest mould and place it on a lace paper covered cake stand, then take the largest ring of the smaller mould and place it on top of the first one, in this way continue by taking one ring of each mould at a time until you get to the top.

FOR BEEHIVES—All one size rings are used until you come to the roof, the roof is then tapered off with the smaller rings, all these kinds of ornaments are decorated with sugar roses, flowers, paper leaves, gum leaves, icing etc.

A very slight practice will enable anyone to improve and invent simular designs such as, flower baskets, fruit baskets, wells, etc., to numerous to mention. Complete set,   -   -   - $2.00

THE LETTER AND FIGURE MOULD.

This handy mould contains the full alphabet, punctuations and figures, the letters are three-quarters of an inch, and the figures half inch high size of mould 6 x 3½ inch. The impressions are intended to lay on top of large cakes in shape of thus: "Happy New Year," Merry Christmas," etc.

DIRECTIONS—Traganth paste or gelatine paste is generally pressed in and cut even with the mould, by putting a little mucilage or molasses on the end of your fore finger, the impressions can easily be removed from the mould by touching them at the back.

See "The Art of Baking," how easy the above pastes are made.   -   -   -   .   - $1.00

"KNOWLEDGE IS POWER."

PATENT CHARLOTTE-RUSSE PANS.

Advantage over old style.

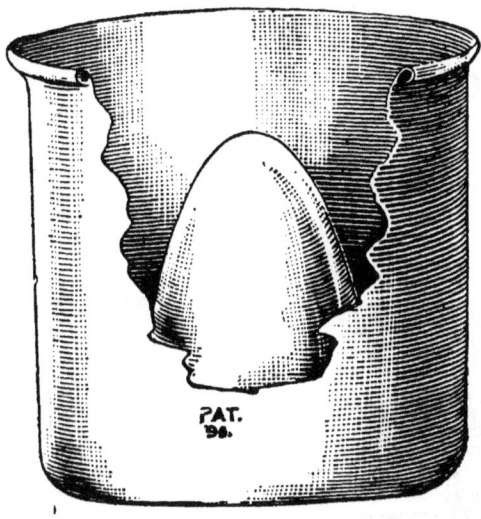

No paper cups are needed, no sponge cake sheets to be baked, no cutting nor trimming, no leakage, no waste, no lining of paper cups.

No laying out with lady fingers.

Simply fill the pans with sponge cake mixture, when baked remove them from the pans, and fill them with whipped cream. The cake itself forms a regular cup with large hole in centre to receive the cream, these pans will pay for themselves in a very short time, 15 cents each, $1.50 per dozen.

VIENNA ROLL STAMP.

This stamp does away with all the difficulties of making vienna rolls, it may also be used for hot cross buns; it is a marvel to the practical baker.

DIRECTIONS—For rolls: Stamp the rolls when half proved and turn them over, when three-quarters proved turn them over again, wash over with water and bake in steam oven. For buns: Stamp when half proved. Send by express, $0.25. By mail. $0.30

"SEEING IS BELIEVING."

PATENT JUMBLE APPARATUS.
Perfection the Aim of Invention.

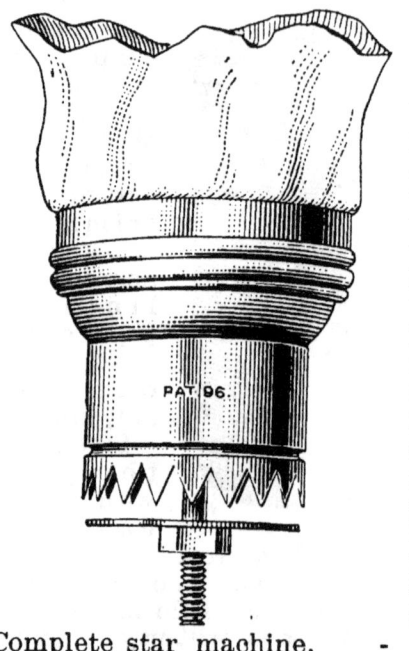

A handy tool for painters and decorators for making plain and fancy rosettes

This tool is a marvel to any one interested in the baking business; it is astonishing how quick and easy a variety of cakes can be brought to its proper shape and size: Such as jumbles, French crullers, kisses meringues, macaroon rings, cream tartlets, etc. The goods made with this tool are seamless, uniform and most beautiful in appearance, any person can operate it to perfection.

Complete star machine. - - - $1.50
" plain " $1.50 [By mail 10c. extra.]

ORNAMENTATION STAMPS.

These little stamps enables any person to make the most difficult designs such as scrolls, console, valutes, etc., which formerly required skilled work-

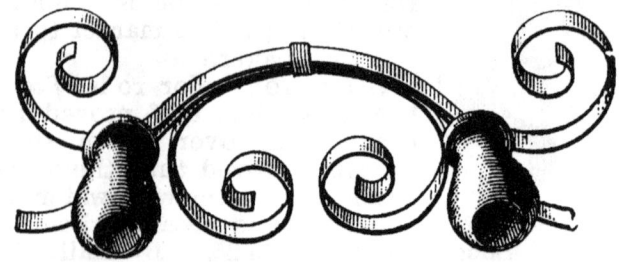

men and long months of study, they are stamped direct on the cake and may be used in the same manner as a rubber stamp. If used on wet icing they should be dipped the least bit in corn starch, on dry icing a pad or pencil may be used.

DIRECTIONS—First find the centre of the cake, then devide the outer edge in as many equal distances to suit the selected design, now stamp the cake in each space on top and sides and follow the marks with the suitable tubes, an ornament or a netting may be placed in the centre and a heavy border around the outer edge of the cake, a number of different designs can be made with one stamp, by reversing and placing them in different positions

Set of twelve stamps all different shapes with book of designs, - - - - - $2.50
Single stamps, - - - - - - .25

Special stamps made to order at the same rates. Send us ten-cents and we will mail you a book of designs, simply to show what beautiful work there can be done with the above stamps.

THE LITTLE ORNAMENTOR.

This tool is designed for very fine work. such as: Writing, making of roses and flowers, the ornamentation of Easter eggs and cards, etc. It consists of a small rubber bag No. 1; one inside screw and s x patent screw tubes. With this tool we send our finest tubes suitable for the above work, if larger or different tubes are wanted it must be stated in the order. They may be selected from our engravings and ordered by the number. Send by express, $1. By mail, $1.10. Single tubes or bag screws 10 cents each, or $1.00 per dozen.

Book of designs free with above.

PATENT RUBBER BULB

For Relief Decoration.

Especially adapted for painters, decorators and relief workers. Our improved apparatus for relief decoration, consist of an elastic cyclinder, closed at one end; made of pure India rubber, an electro-plated screw socket is securely fastened at its lower open end to receive the different ornamenting tubes. This bulb will out last dozens of the common confectioners bags; it is filled from the bottom the same as our ornamen ing syringe; any part can be duplicated at a small cost. The rubber bulb, $1. With 1 dozen electro-plated brass tubes, $2. With 2 dozen electro plated brass tubes, 2 50. If sent by mail, 10 cents extra.

Book of designs free with above.

"Be as careful of the property of others as you would of your own."

"MADE WITH THE SCROLL AND RING MOULDS."

It will pay you to change show pieces weekly and to store the old ones for future use.

"MADE WITH THE SCROLL AND RING MOLDS."

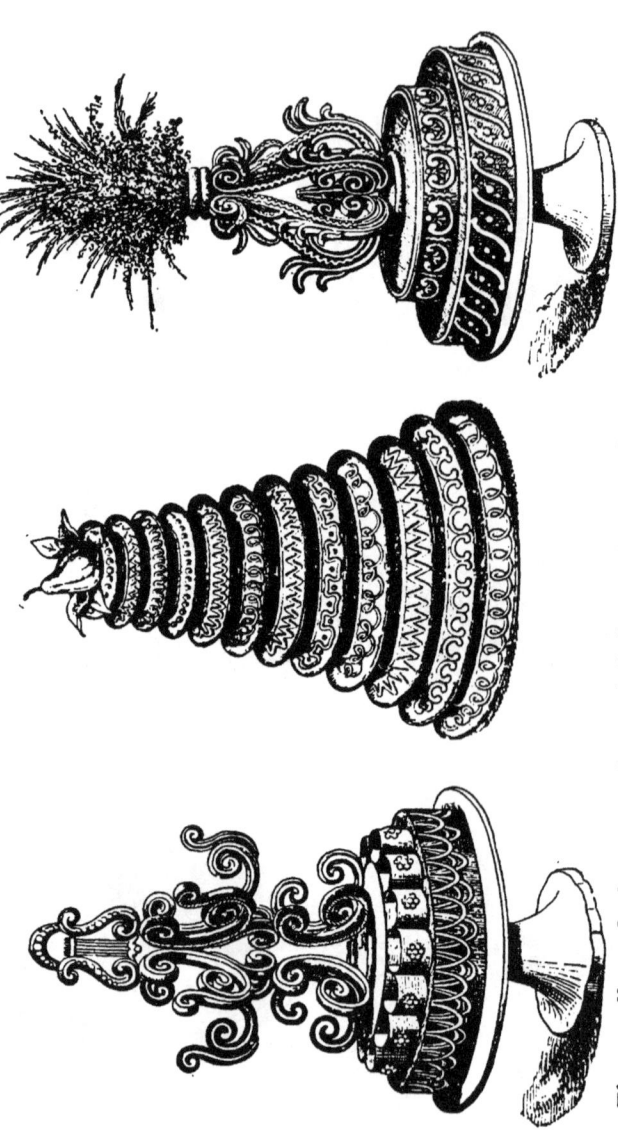

The scrolls and rings may be casted from plaster of paris, and the cakes imitated through a cheese box, that is if made for show only. Try it, it will pay

"MADE WITH RING MOLDS AND THE ORNAMENTATION STAMPS."

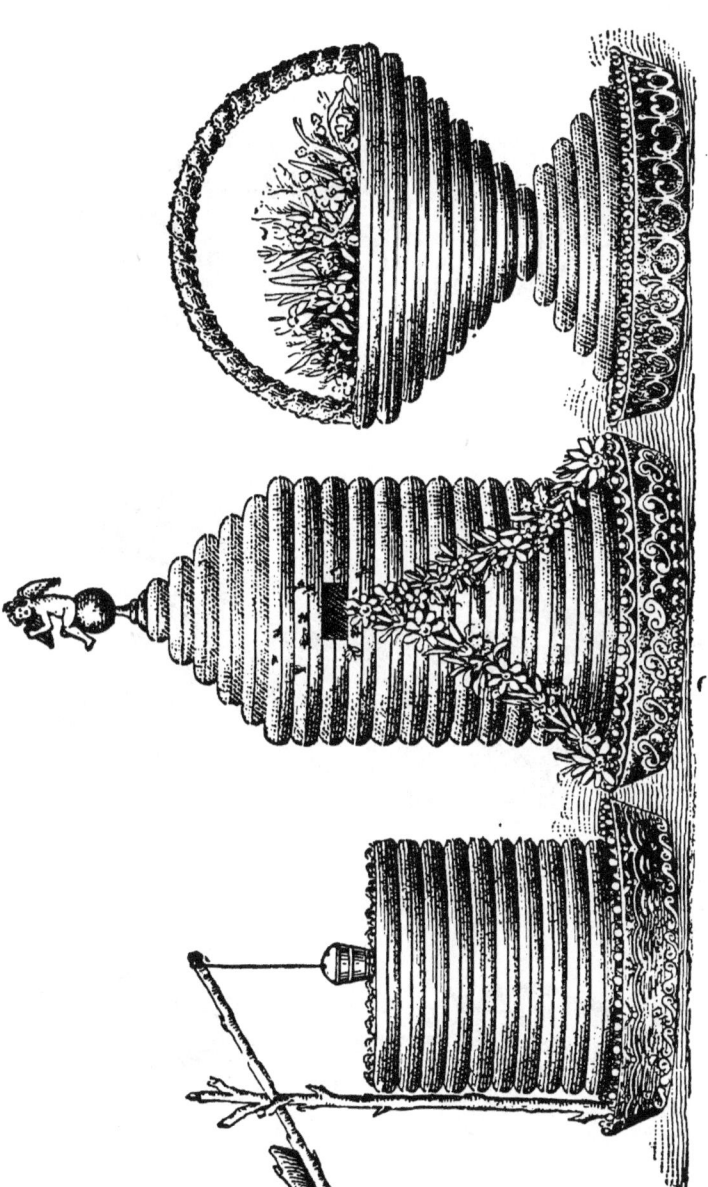

An body can make them in one hours' time. If made of plaster paris they will not cost 25 cents. And see what

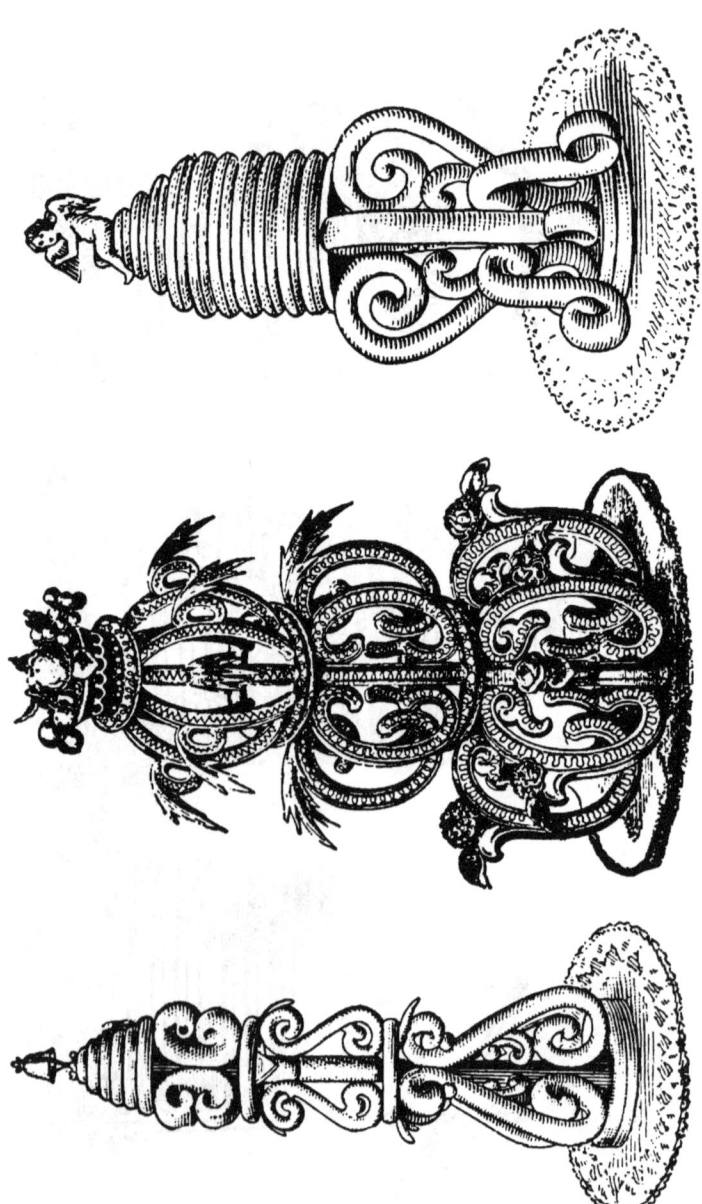

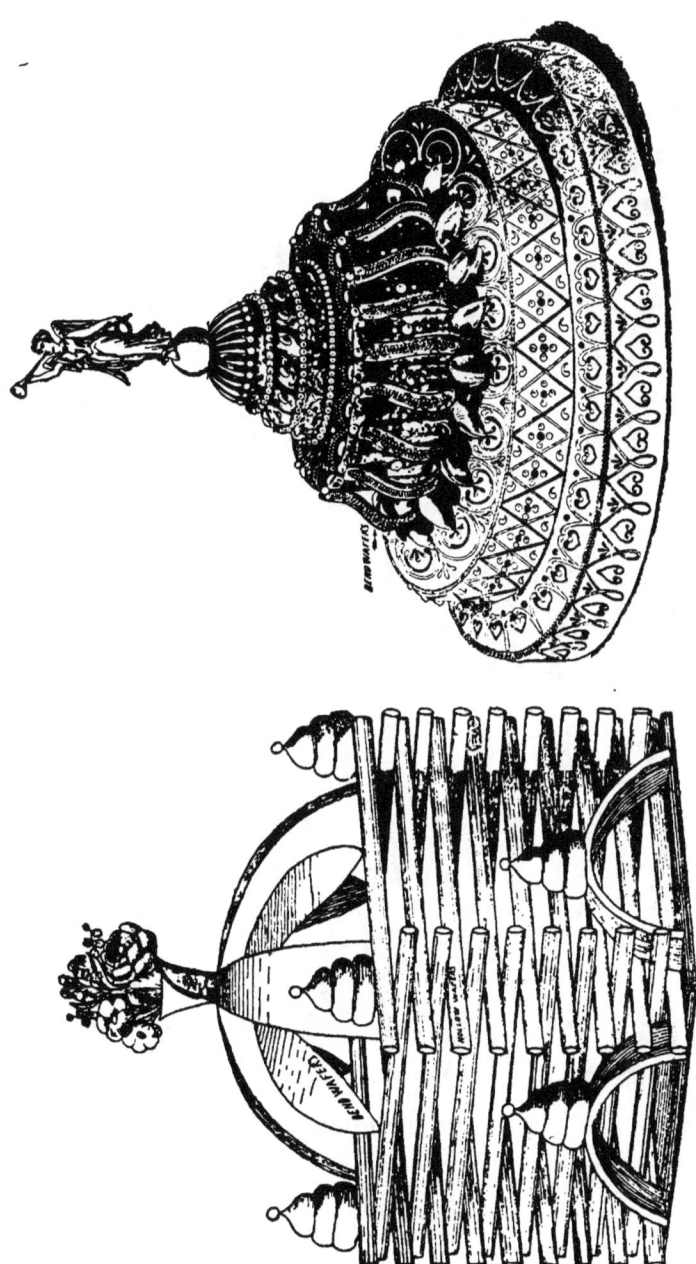

BRASS ORNAMENTING TUBES.

These Tubes are seamless and without screw, and are not equalled by any in the market.

Price,.......$1.00 per dozen or 10 cents each.

Book of Designs free with one dozen tubes.

$1.00   Each.

Case Fryers.

Saucer.   Oval.   Diamond.   Cup.
3½   3½x2¼   3½x2¼   2¼ inches.
Each 1½ inches deep.

PERFECT JUMBLE SET.

Only one bag required in the shop, as tubes are interchangeable and can be changed instantly.

Complete with Bag and Recipe Book, $1.00.

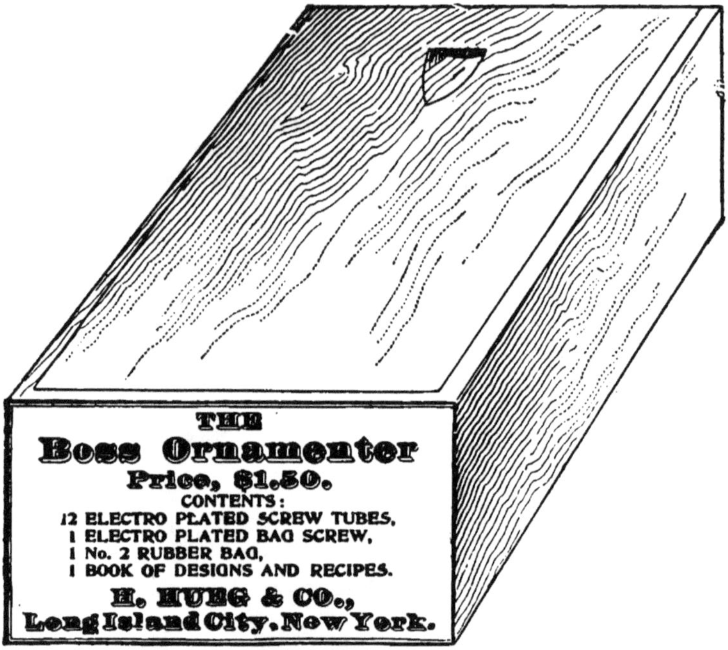

THE
Boss Ornamenter
Price, $1.50.
CONTENTS:
12 ELECTRO PLATED SCREW TUBES,
1 ELECTRO PLATED BAG SCREW,
1 No. 2 RUBBER BAG,
1 BOOK OF DESIGNS AND RECIPES.

H. HUEG & CO.,
Long Island City, New York.

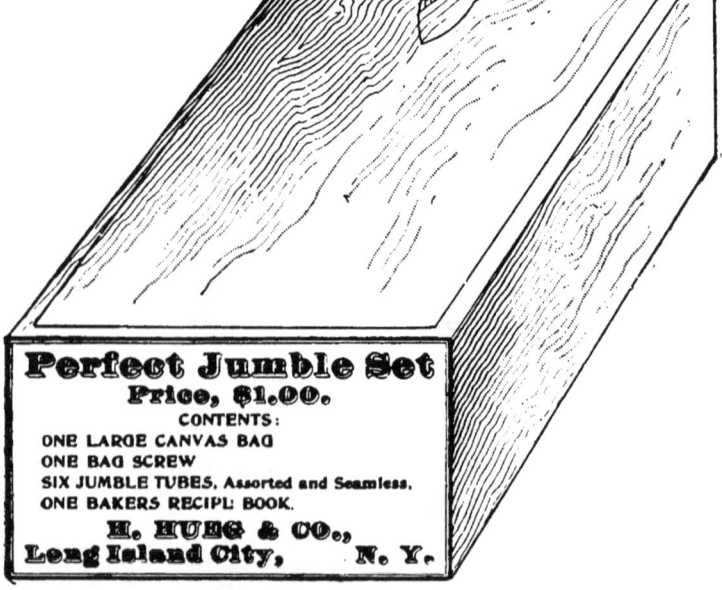

Perfect Jumble Set
Price, $1.00.
CONTENTS:
ONE LARGE CANVAS BAG
ONE BAG SCREW
SIX JUMBLE TUBES, Assorted and Seamless.
ONE BAKERS RECIPE BOOK.

H. HUEG & CO.,
Long Island City,   N. Y.

Prints taken from some of the Ornamentation Stamps.

The following designs explain how to use the Ornamentation Stamps. After you have the prints it is an easy matter to trace them with tube and bag, and finish them to perfection.

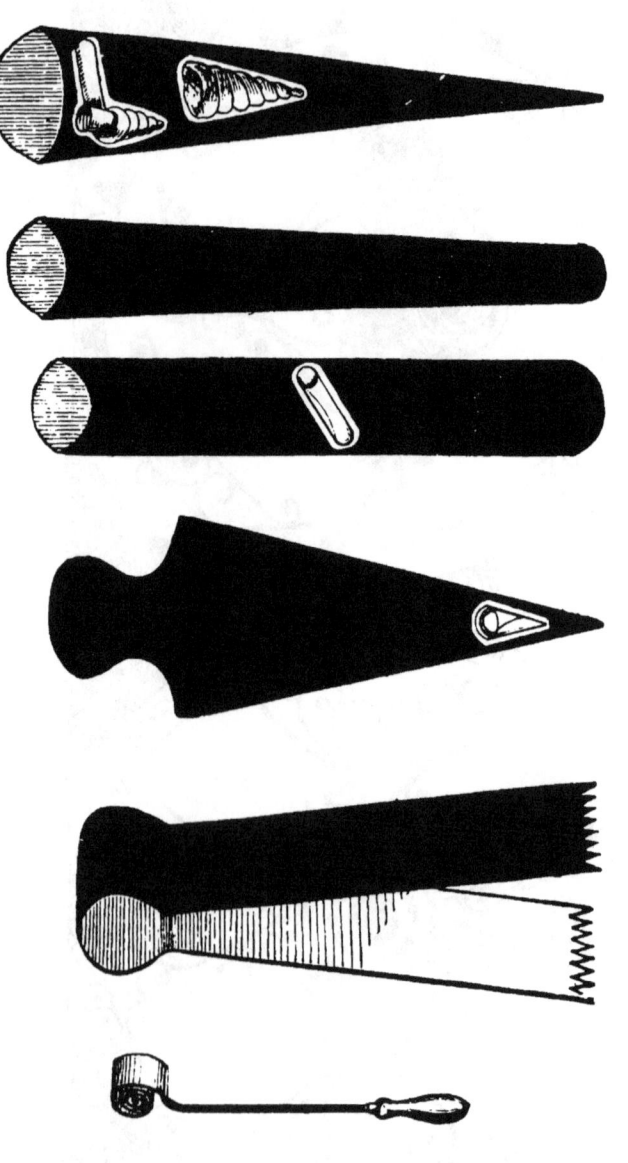

No. 1—Sprungfeder-Eisen, $1.50. No. 2—Paste Knipper, 15 cents. No. 3—Wood Turning for Cornucopias, 50 cents per dozen. No. 4—Wood Turning for Brandy Snaps and Almond Wafers, 50 cents per dozen. No. 5 and 6 are Tin Tubes for Cream Rolls and Schiller Locken, $1.00 per dozen.

METAL STENCILS FOR CAKE DECORATION.

A boy can ornament six layer cakes in one minute.

DIRECTIONS.—Place the Stencil on top of a layer cake iced with either chocolate or water icing, then sift a little xxxx sugar on top of the stencil and remove the stencil carefully. Stock Stencils are 10 inches in diameter, but we make any size to order.

Price, 50c. each. Twelve different designs.

ILLUSTRATIONS.

1, 2, 3 and 4 shows how the Rose is made. 5, 6, 7 and 8 shows how the Narcissus the Dahlia and the Pansy is made.

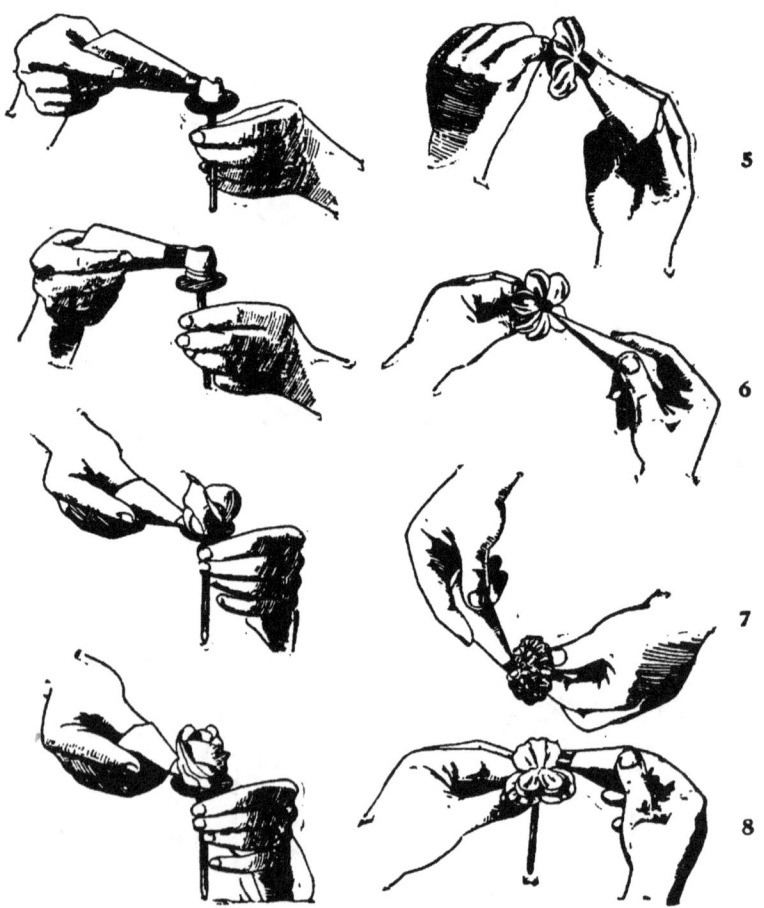

How the Different Flowers are Made.

For drying the flowers, place the nails in a pan of granulated sugar, or coarse corn meal; or a board with little holes bored into it may be used. Paper cornets with and without tubes are generally used for making flowers.

HOW TO MAKE THE ROSE.

Besides a well beaten icing it is necessary to have a fine set of tubes, about two dozen of flower nails, some ornamenting paper and a flat pan filled with granulated sugar or corn meal.

The first operation is to put a star in centre of about one dozen flower nails, this is done to give them a little chance to dry, so that they will stand the resistance of the second operation of the rose tube; next take your paper cornet with the rose tube inserted in the right hand and the flower nail in the left hand, and as you press the cornet you will find the icing curl round, as seen in the illustration No. 1, turn the nail round at the same time you press the cornet, and as you coil the ribbon of icing be careful to keep the centre open and not allow it to look too solid (Fig. 2 shows how the centre is raised for large roses); this is the second operation, say on about a dozen nails, then pick up the first one, which has had a chance to dry a little, and put on the loose leaves in a circular twist motion by having the convex side of the tube facing the nail head, as shown in Figs. 3 and 4; in this way continue.

Figures 5, 6, 7 and 8 shows how the Narcissus, the Dahlia and the Pansy are made; the illustrations explain themselves and the reader will know by this time how to go to work.

Flower Tubes, One Dollar per dozen.
Flower Nails, Fifty Cents per dozen.
Ornamenting Paper, One Cent per sheet.

HOW TO USE OUR CARD BOARD PATTERNS.

Flower Nails, 50 cents per dozen.

Please study the white dots on this engraving. The fields of this star may be filled with jelly of different colors and the netting placed on top of jelly.

ILLUSTRATIONS.

No. 1. Hold the knife steady and turn the cake.
No. 2 shows how to make a proper paper cornet.
No. 3 shows how to make roses. First put a star in the center of the nail head, then add the leaves as shown in cut. The trick of making roses lies in the turning of the nail.

CARDBOARD PATTERNS FOR CAKE DECORATIONS.

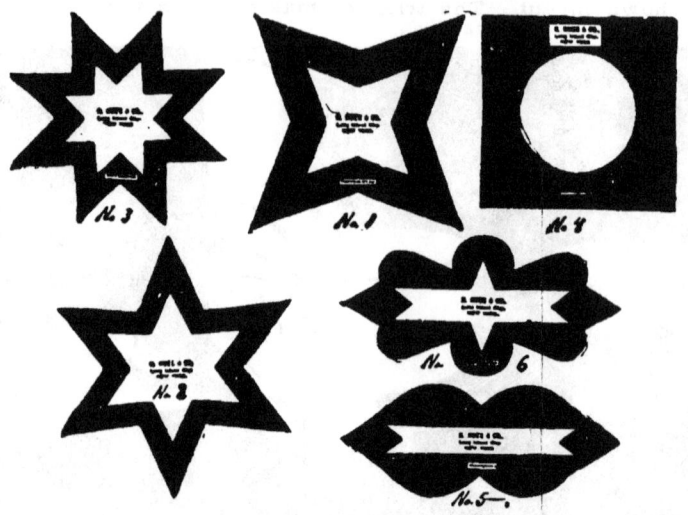

The advantage of using these patterns is not only by drawing a pencil mark around its edges, but it is mostly the easy way in which cake tops can be divided in equal distances; this is the most important point in decorating.

For instance:—With the above 6 pointed star a cake can be laid out in 2, 3, 4, 6 and 12 points; these points are the foundation from which all designs are worked out. Say 2 opposite points in an oval, 3 points in a triangle, (take every other point) 4 points in a diamond, (take two inside and two outside points) 6 points in a hexagon, 12 points in a 6 pointed star. All other patterns are used in a similar way, after a little practice the reader will find that he cannot be without them. Printed directions will be furnished with every set.

Set of six Cardboard Patterns assorted and regular size. Price 50 cents.

STAMPS FOR CAKE
ORNAMENTATION.
PRICE, - - - - - $2.50.
CONTENTS:
15 ASSORTED STAMPS FOR CAKE ORNAMENTATION,
6 CARDBOARD PATTERNS FOR CAKE CENTRES,
1 BOOK OF DESIGNS,
1 BOOK OF RECIPES AND INSTRUCTIONS.
H. HUEG & CO.
Long Island City, New York.

THE
LITTLE ORNAMENTOR.
PRICE, - - - - - - $1.00.
CONTENTS:
ONE RUBBER BAG, SIZE No. 1,
ONE PAT. SILVERPLATED BAG SCREW,
SIX PAT. SCREW TUBES, ASSORTED.
H. HUEG & CO., Long Island City, New York.

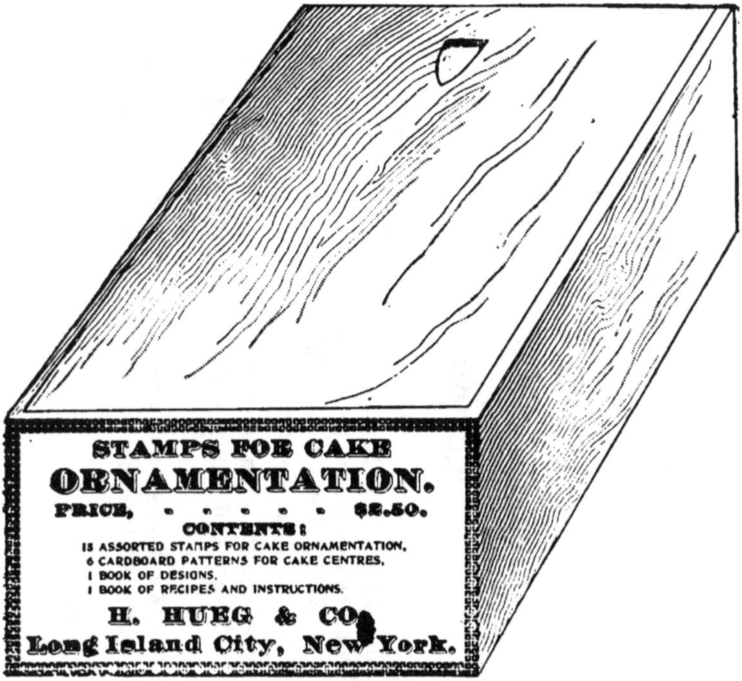

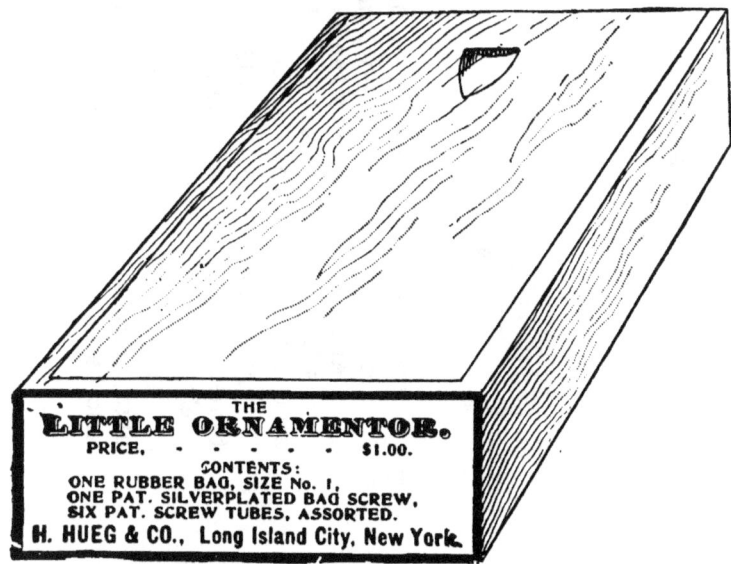

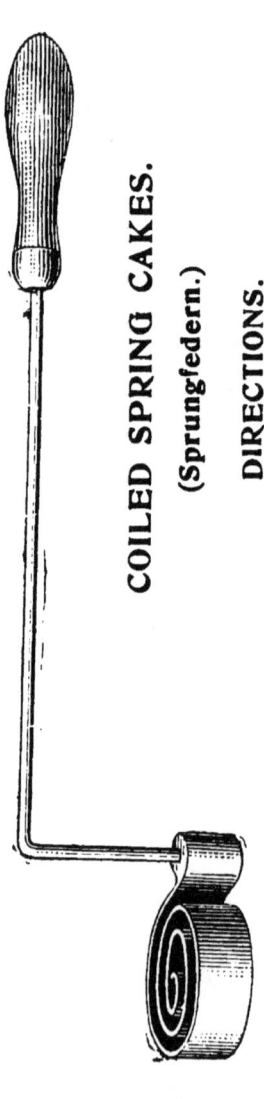

COILED SPRING CAKES.
(Sprungfedern.)
DIRECTIONS.

The above tool is used in the same manner as the Case Fryers. Heat the iron in the boiling grease—when hot, dip it into the batter almost to the upper edge and back again into the boiling grease, bake to a golden color—knock the iron a little and a perfect COILED SPRING CAKE will fall off—turn them over and dust them with a mixture of Sugar and Cinnamon.

These Cakes can be sold at 1 cent each with 90 per cent. profit—and customers will be well pleased with the large and tasty Cakes they are getting for their money.

BATTER—Mix 1½ pound of flour, 6 ounces of sugar and 1 pint of milk in a high, narrow basin, add 10 beaten eggs and mix thoroughly. This batter can also be used for Case Fryers.

Price, $1.50 Each.

CARDBOARD STENCILS FOR FANCY WAFERS.

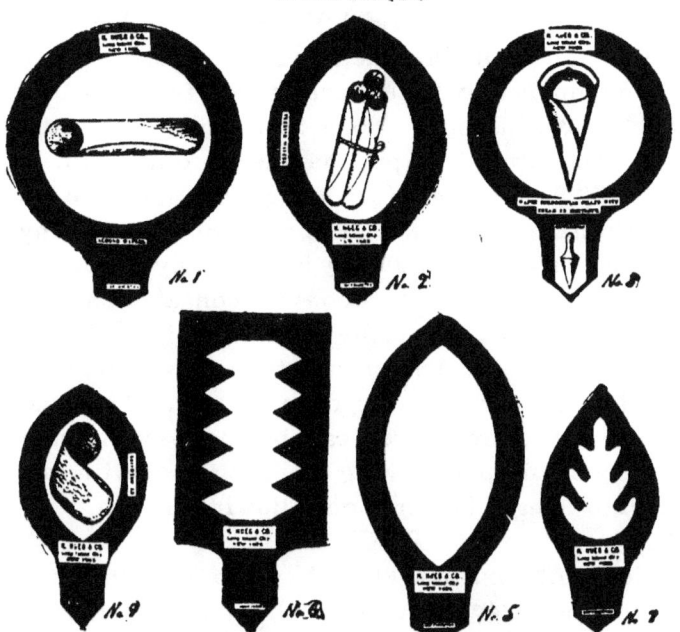

Directions for Prepairing and Using our Cardboard Stencils.

How to cut them.—When cutting out the stencils care should be taken that the *in* as well as the outside edges are nice and smooth; a sharp pointed pen-knife may be used to cut out the center piece while a pair of scissors will answer for cutting the outer edge, the stencils are then ready for shaping a variety of fancy wafers.

How to use them.—Place the stencil on a waxed or lightly greased pan, then take a little dough on the point of a pallet knife and fill in the inner space one-sixteenth inch thick, repeat as often as required and bake them in a hot oven, as soon as they leave the oven they are cut loose and bent into the desired shape.

How to roll and bend them.—No. 1 Almond Wafers are rolled over round sticks 1 in. thick and 6 in. long. No. 2 Turkish Wafers are rolled over round sticks ¾ in. thick and 6 in. long. No. 3 Cornucopias are rolled over taper turnings 1 in. thick and 4 in. long. No. 4 St. Germains are bent to a semi-circle on a peel handle or rolling pin.

Nos. 5, 6 and 7 are for show pieces and cake decorations. They can be bent into almost any shape; an ogee moulding is generally used, but they may be bent into a convex, concave, square, circle, oval, etc. to suit the selected design. These wafers are generally ornamented and will be found most useful for elevating cake centers. The most attractive show pieces can be made with these wafers by simply sticking them together with caramel or icing. See cuts on following pages.

RECIPES.

No. 1, Almond Wafers.—Mix 1 lb Almond Paste, 12 whites, 1½ lb sugar, ½ lb flour, 1 gill cream, little salt and cinnamon.

No. 2, Turkish Wafers.—Mix 1 lb almond paste, 6 eggs, 1¼ lb sugar, 5 oz corn starch, ½ gill rose water, little salt and nutmeg.

No. 3, Cornucopias.—Mix 1 lb almond paste, 1 lb sugar, ½ pt yelks, 1 gill cream, 6 oz flour, little salt, cinnamon and vanilla.

No. 4, St. Germains.—Mix ½ lb almond paste, ½ pt whites, ½ lb sugar, 2 oz flour, little sherry wine, salt, mace and cinnamon, strew shredded almond on top.

The following recipe is used for Nos. 5, 6 and 7—Mix ½ lb almond paste, ¾ lb sugar, 2 oz flour, 5 whites, little water, salt and cinnamon.

Complete set of seven assorted stencils, 50 cents.

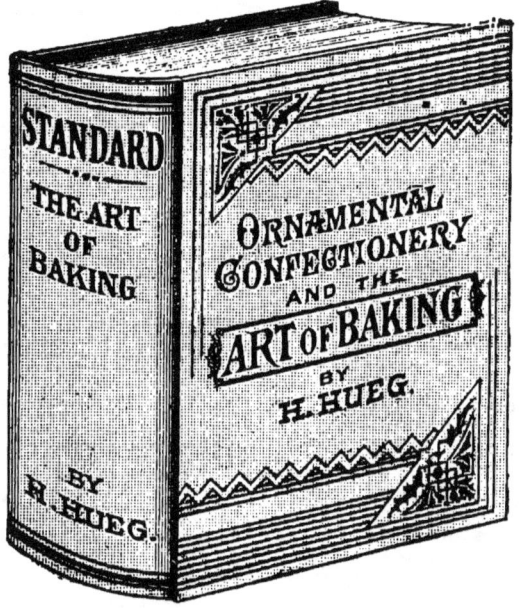

30,000 Copies sold in the United States.

Printed in English and German.

Price $2.50.

The above is the only reliable bakers' receipe book in existence, it has been the first one ever published in the United States, and is continually growing, it is out in its Sixth Edition.

"**We guarantee every receipe in this book.**"

Pick me up at your leisure there may be $ $ $ $ inside for you.

A WARNING.

Anyone intending to buy a bakers' receipe book should write to us, because all the receipe books ever published we keep in stock and are ready for shipment, but many of them sailing under a false flag, others are made up by newspaper men, hotel bakers' and other men who do not know how a bakershop looks during the night or day, write to us and we will give you all the information free of charge, we find that this is necessary as we know that many bakers' have been disappointed by buying a worthless book.

A book full of puddings and sauces will not answer for the practical baker. Enclose a two-cent stamp.

PRICE LIST OF PATENT TOOLS.

The Standard Cake Filler	$5.00
Improved Patent Cake Filler	2.50
The Handy Rock Cake Stamp	.25
Improved Candy Funnel	1.50
Pie Stamps, each	.25
Improved Ornamenting Syringe	1.50
Stamps for Cake Ornamentation	2.50
The Little Ornamentor	1.00
The Boss Ornamentor	1.50
The Scroll Mould	2.50
The Ring Mould	2.00
The Letter and Figure Mould	1.00
Patent Charlotte Russe Moulds, per dozen	1.50
Vienna Roll Stamp, each	.25
Patent Jumble Apparatus	1.50
Patent Rubber Relief Bulb	1.00
Seamless Ornamenting Tubes, without Screw, per dozen	1.00
Seamless Ornamenting Tubes, with Screw, per dozen	1.00
Bag Screws, each	.10
Case Fryers, each	1.00
All kinds of Cake Cutters, each	.25
Shrewsbury Cake Cutter and mold	.50
Perfect Jumble Set, Complete with Bag	1.00
Card-board Stencils, for Fancy Wafers, per set of 7	.50
Sprungfeder Eisen (Coiled Spring Cake Iron)	1.50
Paste Nipper	.15
Wood Turnings, for Cornucopias, per dozen	.50
Wood Turnings, for Brandy Snaps, per dozen	.50
Tin Tubes, for Cream Rolls, per dozen	1.00
Metal Stencils for Cake Decorations, each	.50
Card-board Patterns for Cake Decoration, per set of 6	.50
Flower Nails, per dozen	.50
Ornamenting Paper, per sheet	.01

Prices on Single Parts of Our Cream Fillers.

The Coiled Spring	.10
The Cast-Iron Triangle Cross Bar	.25
The Washer	.05
The Nut	.05
The Cast-Iron Plunger only	.15
The Plunger Rod, with Knob and Gauge	.50
The Nickel-Plated Cutting and Filling Tube	.25

Any of the above tools or part of them will be sent upon receipts of price by

H. HUEG.

Cor. Thomson Ave. and L. I. R. R., Long Island City, N. Y. One block from Court House.

Patent Bag Screws for Brass Ornamenting Tubes.

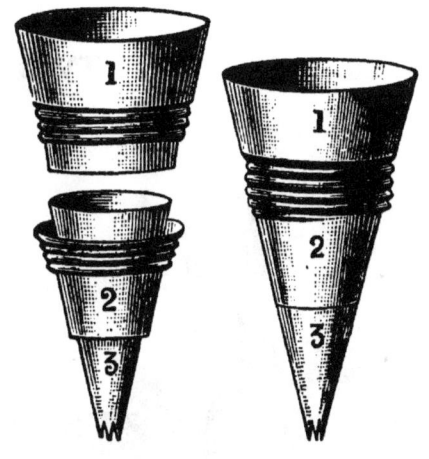

Complete Outfit, consisting of 1 Bag Screw, 1 No. 2 Rubber Bag and 12 Assorted Brass Tubes,

PRICE, $1.00

Will mail this Bag Screw to any address on receipt of 10 Cents.

Patent Cottage Stamp.

Great Time and Labor Saver.

PRICE, $1.50.   **TWO SIZES.**

DIRECTIONS.

In place of moulding the Cottage in six pieces, mould them in one piece, place same in pans, when half raised dust them lightly with Rye flour and stamp with the above tool.

PATENT RELIEF BULB.

THE BULB ONLY $1.00.

With One Dozen Tubes,	- -	$2.00
With Two Dozen Tubes,	- -	$2.50

Our tube engravings you will find on another page, from which you select.

Ice Cream Cone Fryer, $2.50

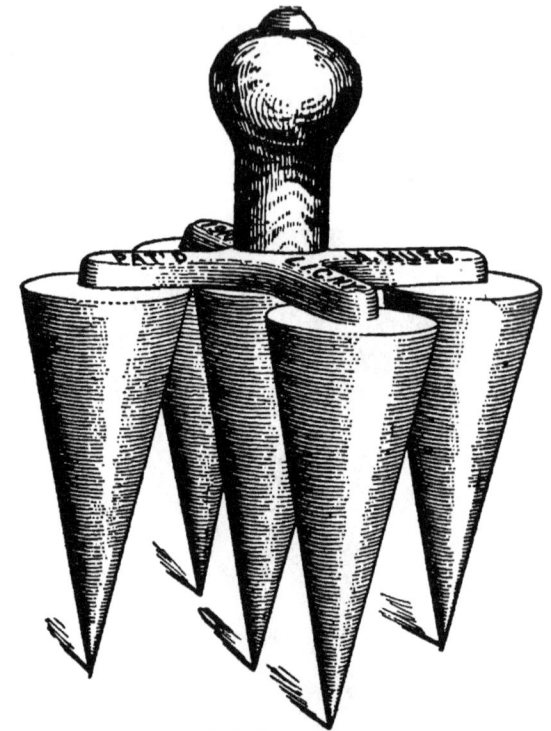

Directions:

Heat the iron in the boiling grease; dip into the batter and back into the fat; fry to a golden color.

BATTER: 1 lb. soft flour, 4 ozs. C sugar, ¾ pt. dis. eggs, ¾ pt. milk. Mix flour and sugar and eggs with an egg beater very good, then add the milk gradually. In the meantime have your oil heated to 370 to 375 degrees. Put your spring iron in the oil, allow to get hot; then dip the iron into the mixture, but don't let the mixture run over the iron. Then take the iron out and put in the heated oil; in a few seconds the cake is baked. Take out and give it a knock on a piece of wood to remove the cake from the iron. Put the iron in the oil again for a few seconds, knock the adhering oil off, and continue the same way as before. Should the mixture become thick, add a little more milk and eggs. This cake requires a little experience, but it is a nice showy cake, which has a fine taste, if eaten fresh, but it will be dry the next day.

CONFECTIONERS' BAGS.

No. 1, 2, 3, 4, 5, 6, of bag
Size, 10 in., 13 in., 16-in , 22 in., 24-in., 28-in., l'ght
Price, 20c., 30c., 40c., 50c., 60c., 75c. each

All baker supply houses sell our goods, but be sure and ask for "Hueg's Patent Tools," and take no other. We guarantee our goods to be the best in the market. H. Hueg is a practical baker and confectioner of large experience and understands the wants of bakers.

We would rather refund money than allow dissatisfaction.

Our rigid terms—prepay or C. O. D.—will be compensated by the excellent quality and cheapness of goods, and quick delivery.

Cash may be sent by express or postal money orders, small amounts in one or two-cent stamps. Checks and drafts payable to

H. HUEG, Long Island City, N. Y.

All goods ordered sent by mail, will be sent at purchaser's risk. Oblige us with your orders and you will find we serve you faithfully.

Low prices. Quick forwarding. Excellent quality.

LIST OF TRADE BOOKS.

For Bread & Cake Bakers.

The Art of Baking, 230 p.p. cloth, by H. Hueg $2.50
" " " paper cover " $2.00
Illustrirtes Cake & Conditor Buch..... " $1.00
The Illustrated Cake Baker, paper cover " $ .50
Condensed Treatise on the Art of Baking " $ .50
The Complete Bread, Cake & Cracker Baker by
J. Thomson Gill $3.00
The Complete Practical Pastry Cook " " $3.00
New Book of Designs by H. Hueg...........$ .50
The Champion Cracker Baker by P. F. Carroll..$2.00

For Confectioners.

The Practical Confectioner by H. Hueg.......$1.50
The Little Confectioner by H. Hueg... ....$ .50
The Complete Practical Confectioner, J. T. Gill $3.00
The Complete Practical Ornamentor " " $4.00
Ornamental Confectionery by H. Hueg......$2.50

For Stewards and Cooks.

Whitehead's Stewards Hand Book...........$3.00
" Hotel Meat Cooking............$2.00
" American Pastry Cook..........$2.00
" Cooking for Profits.............$3.00
Meister's Vest Pocket Pastry Cook.............$1.00
Fellow's Selection of Dishes.................$1.00
Fellow's Chefs Reminder $1.00
Lempke's Desserts and Salads...............$1.50
Lempke's Meat Cooking for Hotels & Private $2.50

All of the above books will be sent upon receipt of price by

H. HUEG

Cor. Thomson Ave. and L. I. R. R.

One Block from Court House, Long Island City, N. Y.

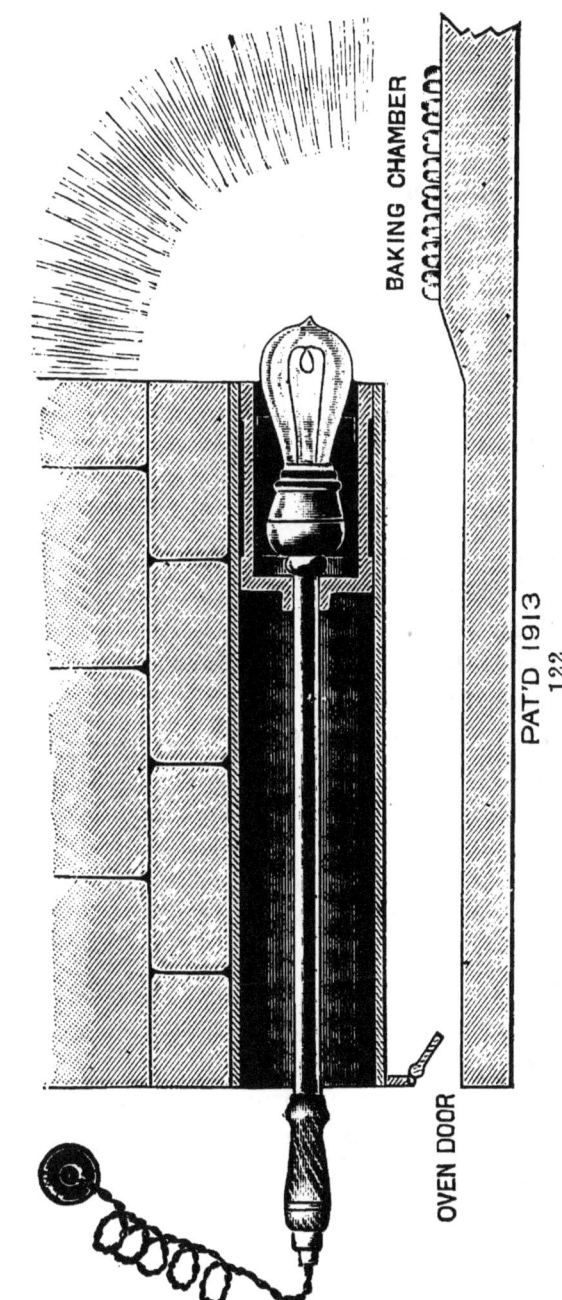

INDEX.

	PAGES.
Almond Bar	19
Almond Cream	33
Almond Cream Chocolate	33
Almond Cream Rose	34
Artificial Fruit Essence	62
American Cream	69
Almonds, Milk of	70
Bon Bons	48
Bon Bons, Chocolate	42
Bon Bons, Coffee	42
Bon Bons, Cognac	42
Bon Bons, Vanilla	48
Bon Bons, Almonds	49
Bon Bons, Chocolate	50
Blanc Mange	69
Blanc Mange, Old-Fashioned	70
Burnt Sugar	75
Caramel Ornaments	10
Caramels, Vanilla	14
Caramels, Vanilla	15
Caramels, Maple	16
Caramels, Chocolate	16
Caramels, Chocolate	17
Cocoanuts	20
Cocoanut Cakes	20
Cocoanut Cream Bar	21
Cream for Chocolate Drops	21
Chocolate Cream Drops	22
Chocolate Cream Bar	23

PAGES.

Combination Cream Bar	24
Candy Sticks and Drops	27
Candy, Cut Drops	29
Candy Cream	30
Chocolate Paste	32
Cream Walnuts	34
Clarifying	3
Crystalization	4
Cream Dates	35
Cream Figs	35
Candied Nuts	35
Crystalization	37
Cough Candy	38
Cough Candy, Good	41
Cream Chocolate, Italian	43
Cream, Italian White	44
Colors that are not Poisonous	46
Colors, to make	47
Colors, Yellow	47
Colors, Red	47
Colors, Blue	47
Charlotte Russe	68
Cream, American	69
Cream, Bavarian	71
Easter Egg	6
Essential Oils and Extracts	57
Extract Anise	58
Extract Cloves	58
Extract Cinnamon	58
Extract Bitter Almonds	58
Extract Ginger	58

PAGES.

Extract Sarsaparilla 58
Extract Capsicum 59
Extract Vanilla, 1........................59
Extract Vanilla and Tonka, 2...............60
Extract Vanilla, 3........................60
Extract of Vanilla from the Dry Bean........60
Extract of Lemon 61
Extract of Peppermint 61
Extract of Wintergreen....................62
Egg Nogg 72
Gum Arabic Drops........................41
Gold Web 7
Hore Hound Candy........................38
Introduction 2
Ice Cream Candy, Vanilla 8
Ice Cream Candy..........................12
Ice Cream Candy, Strawberry...............14
Ice Cream Candy, Chocolate................13
Italian Cream Candy, Chocolate............43
Italian Cream Candy, Vanilla..............44
Ice Cream Vanilla........................62
Ice Cream, Vanilla Chocolate..............63
Ice Cream, Lemon........................64
Ice Cream, Strawberry....................65
Ice Cream, Raspberry....................65
Ice Cream, Custard........................65
Ice Cream; Improvement, Custard and Cream.66
Ice Cream, cheap..........................66
Ice Cream, Bisque........................66
Ice Cream, Parisienne Coffee..............67
Ice Cream, Coffee........................67

	PAGES.
Icing for Confectionery and Cake	71
Icing for Cake	72
Imitation Eggs in Grained Sugar	7
Lemon Acid Drops	25
Lemon Drops, without acid	26
List of Tools	3
Lozenge, General Directions	73
Meringue Kisses	72
Molasses Candy, light	31
Molasses Candy, Old-Fashioned	31
Milk of Almonds	70
Papier Mache	11
Peanut Bar	18
Philadelphia Walnut Candy	24
Pop Corn Balls	40
Powder Sugar, Red	44
Powder Sugar, Yellow	44
Powder Sugar, Green	45
Poisonous Colors	45
Panorama Eggs	8
Pastilage	11
Rock Candy	36
Rock Sugar	11
Rose, how to make	105
Sarsaparilla Taffy	35
Sponge Sugar or Spanish Candy	39
Spinach Green	45
Spun Sugar	7
Silver Web	6
Sugar Spinning	5
Syrup, Simple	50

	PAGES.
Syrup, Raspberry	50
Syrup, Strawberry	51
Syrup, Pineapple	52
Syrup, Pineapple, artificial	52
Syrup, Sarsaparilla	52
Syrup, Cream No. 1	53
Syrup, Cream No. 2	53
Syrup, Cream No. 3	53
Syrup, Cream, Imitation	54
Syrup, Chocolate	54
Syrup, Coffee	54
Syrup, Ginger	55
Syrup, Sherbert	55
Syrup, Orgeat	55
Syrup, Orgeat True	55
Syrup, Strawberry Imitation	56
Syrup, Raspberry Imitation	56
Syrup, Milk Punch	56
Syrup, Wine	56
Taffy Candy	32
Taffy, Everton Candy	32
Taffy, Cinnamon Candy	35
Taffy, Sarsaparilla Candy	35
Thermometer	3

TOOLS FOR BAKERS.

Boss Ornamentor	84
Cake Fillers	80
Candy Funnel	81
Charlotte Russe Pans	88
Case Fryers	98

PAGES.

Cake Patterns	109
Confectioners' Bags	120
Electric Bake Oven Light	122
Ice Cream Cone Fryers	119
Jumble Apparatus	89
Jumble Tubes	98
Letter Mould	87
Little Ornamentor	90
List of Tools	115
List of Trade Books	121
Metal Stencils	104
Ornamenting Syringe	82
Ornamentation Stamps	89, 100, 101, 102
Ornamenting Tubes	97
Patent Bag Screw	116
Patent Cottage Stamp	117
Patent Relief Bulb	118
Pie Stamp	81
Ring Designs	94
Ring Mould	86
Rock Cake Stamp	80
Rose Nails	107
Rubber Bulb	91
Shrewsbury Mould	83
Scroll Mould	85
Scroll Designs	92, 93, 95
Sprungfedern	111
Sugar Roses	105, 106, 107, 108
Viennà Roll Stamp	88
Wood Turnings	103
Wafer Designs	96
Wafer Recipes	113
Wafer Stencils	112